GREAT WINDOWS & WALLS COLLECTION

Meredith® Books
Des Moines, Iowa

MW00974863

Great Windows and Walls Collection
Project Manager/Writer: Heidi Tyline King
Contributing Researcher: Shelley Stewart
Graphic Designer: Sundie Ruppert, Studio G
Copy Chief: Terri Fredrickson
Publishing Operations Manager: Karen Schirm
Senior Editor, Asset and Information Manager: Phillip Morgan
Edit and Design Production Coordinator: Mary Lee Gavin
Editorial Assistant: Kaye Chabot
Book Production Managers: Pam Kvitne, Marjorie J. Schenkelberg, Rick von Holdt, Mark Weaver
Contributing Copy Editor: Amanda Knief
Contributing Proofreaders: Beth Havey, Paula Reece, Nancy Ruhling
Cover Photographer: Tria Giovan
Contributing photographers: Pieter Estersohn Photography (page 249), Alise O'Brien (pages 16–17, 22, 96–99, 259, 266)
Indexer: Sharon Duffy

Meredith® Books
Executive Director, Editorial: Gregory H. Kayko
Executive Director, Design: Matt Strelecki
Senior Editor/Group Manager: Vicki Leigh Ingham
Senior Associate Design Director: Mick Schnepf
Marketing Product Manager: Tyler Woods

Publisher and Editor in Chief: James D. Blume
Editorial Director: Linda Raglan Cunningham
Executive Director, Sales: Ken Zagor
Director, Operations: George A. Susral
Director, Production: Douglas M. Johnston
Director, Marketing: Amy Nichols
Business Director: Jim Leonard

Vice President and General Manager: Douglas J. Guendel

Better Homes and Gardens® **Magazine**
Editor in Chief: Karol DeWulf Nickell
Deputy Editor, Home Design: Oma Blaise Ford

Meredith Publishing Group
President: Jack Griffin
Executive Vice President: Bob Mate

Meredith Corporation
Chairman and Chief Executive Officer: William T. Kerr
President and Chief Operating Officer: Stephen M. Lacy

In Memoriam: E.T. Meredith III (1933-2003)

All of us at Meredith® Books are dedicated to providing you with information and ideas to enhance your home. We welcome your comments and suggestions. Write to us at: Meredith Books, Home Decorating and Design Editorial Department, 1716 Locust St., Des Moines, IA 50309-3023.

If you would like to purchase any of our home decorating and design, cooking, crafts, gardening, or home improvement books, check wherever quality books are sold. Or visit us at: bhgbooks.com

INSPIRED
INTERIORS

Where do you start when you're considering window and wall treatments? Take your decorating cue from the room by using existing design elements as inspiration. Is a particular architectural style evident in the moldings or in the shape of doors and windows? Are there decorative features such as tilework, patterns on the floor, or carved facades of wood or plaster? Do you have furniture that you want to incorporate into the design?

If you like what you see, use it to guide your decisions for wall finishes and window treatments. If you don't, opt for treatments and finishes that disguise design flaws or draw attention away from lackluster features in a room. Window treatments that cover the entire window frame can mask a lack of interesting detail, and wall coverings or faux finishes can imbue an ordinary room with atmosphere. Another way to find the look you want is to clip magazine photos of favorite rooms, walls, and windows. When you have assembled a stack, study the specific styles, textures, and colors that reappear, and weed out the photos that no longer capture your attention. Use these visual cues when shopping to stay true to the look you desire.

Inspiration also comes from accessories, hobbies—even your personality can dictate design. A trip to France might prompt a love for all things Provençal. Your grandmother's lace tablecloth could be the starting point for a Victorian-style dining room, and your seaside vacation might inspire you to bring a nautical theme home.

If your project is complex, enlist the help of an interior designer. These professionals are experienced in working with a number of design styles, and they are trained to listen and extract your best ideas to help you turn them into the reality you envision.

MURAL MASTERPIECE

DAYDREAMS OF A ROMANTIC TRIP TO TUSCANY PROMPTED THE RE-CREATION OF A BEAUTIFULLY DETAILED LIBRARY. FURNISHINGS CONTRIBUTE TO THE STAGING OF THE PERIOD-STYLE DECOR, BUT IT'S THE WALLS AND CEILINGS THAT TRANSFORM THE ENVIRONMENT. ORNATE FRESCOES OF CLASSICAL MOTIFS IN GRAND BAROQUE STYLE ARE "AGED" WITH MUTED UMBERS AND DUSKY YELLOW GLAZES TO RESEMBLE THEIR FADED COUNTERPARTS IN ITALY. WINDOWS INVITE THE OUTDOORS IN AND ARE LEFT BARE, CROWNED AND FRAMED ONLY BY TROMPE L'OEIL MOLDINGS.

Creative Combinations...

LAYERED LOOK A RARELY OPENED WINDOW OUTFITTED WITH PLANTATION SHUTTERS BECOMES, LITERALLY, A FRAME FOR ARTWORK. THE POSITIONINGS ARE UNEXPECTED BUT INTERESTING—A DEPARTURE FROM STANDARD PLACEMENT.

EASY DOES IT Dressing a window doesn't have to be complicated. Take a cue from this fabric designer's studio. A sheer panel hangs on a tension rod that fits inside the window frame. A row of starfish dances across the window at sash height, secured to the panel with glue. For a valance, a sample of his fabric, finished around the edges, is simply tacked to the top of the window frame.

Creative Combinations...

UNUSUAL UTILITY CURTAINS ATTACHED TO SWING-ARM DRAPERY RODS ARE COMMONPLACE, BUT STRETCHING SHEER FABRIC PANELS ON THE SAME RODS TO RESEMBLE FULL-LENGTH SCREENS IS UNCONVENTIONAL AND CREATIVE. TOP AND BOTTOM BORDERS OF GOLD EMBELLISH THE SCREENS BUT KEEP THE LOOK SIMPLE SO THAT ARCHITECTURAL DETAILS AND POLISHED FURNISHINGS DOMINATE THE DECOR.

Creative Combinations...

PAIRED PRESENTATION ALONE, NEITHER A FRINGED CORNICE NOR A TRIO OF SHADES WOULD CAUSE MUCH COMMENT. WHEN COMBINED, HOWEVER, THE TREATMENTS ACCENTUATE THE ROW OF WINDOWS.

CURVACEOUS CONTRAST WIDE HORIZONTAL STRIPES ON THE WALL CARRY THE EYE AROUND THE ROOM. TO BALANCE THAT MOVEMENT, A CURVY CANOPY SUPPORT AND ARCHED CURTAIN ROD DRAW THE EYE UPWARD. THE CUSTOM ROD AND FLOOR-LENGTH DRAPERIES TURN THE ORDINARY WINDOW INTO A FOCAL POINT. TO GIVE DRAPERIES BODY TO STAND OUT FROM THE WALL, CHOOSE STIFF FABRIC AND USE LINING AND INTERLINING.

REFINEMENT IN REVERSE Sheer curtains are usually tucked behind heavy draperies. Here the two swap positions. Understated draperies in dusty blue silk are layered behind luscious printed sheer panels. Each pair hangs on separate rods, allowing them to be drawn separately—the silk panels for privacy and the sheers for filtering light. Layering the sheers on top also brings romantic softness to an eclectic mix of modern and antique furnishings.

Creative Combinations...

SUNRISE, SUNSET VALANCES WITH BOX PLEATS MAKE A STRONG COLOR IMPACT NEAR THE CEILING LINE WITH A FLORAL PRINT WHOSE GROUND MATCHES THE SUNNY WALL COLOR. THE SHEER DRAPERIES REVERSE THE COLOR COMBINATION WITH YELLOW FLOWERS ON A WHITE GROUND. HUNG HIGH ON THE WALL, THE DRAPERIES FORM COLUMNS OF WHITE TO EMPHASIZE THE HEIGHT OF THE CEILING. THE WALL TREATMENT REPRESENTS A LANDSCAPE WITH A PALE BLUE SKY FILLING THE TOP 2 FEET BELOW THE CEILING. A LINE OF DUNES DEFINED BY RED AND BLUE GLAZES DIVIDES THIS BORDER FROM THE GOLDEN WALL BELOW.

Inspiration...

ODE TO ART SHOWCASE A BELOVED PIECE OF ART BY DESIGNING A ROOM TO COMPLEMENT IT. THE CROWN JEWEL OF THIS LIVING ROOM IS OBVIOUS: A DELICATE CHINESE VEST WOVEN FROM BAMBOO BEADS AND DISPLAYED PROMINENTLY ON THE FRENCH COUNTRY-STYLE CHIMNEY BREAST. DISCREET PLANTATION BLINDS AND ANTIQUE LACE PANELS WITH EXTRA-LONG TIES GRACE THE WINDOWS (OPPOSITE). NATURAL LIGHT HIGHLIGHTS THE WALLS, WHICH ARE FAUX FINISHED TO MIMIC FADED FRESCOES ON OLD PLASTER.

Inspiration...

GIFT WRAPPED THE SIGNATURE BLUE COLOR AND WHITE RIBBON OF A TIFFANY GIFT BOX ARE THE IMPETUS BEHIND THIS SITTING ROOM. BELOW THE GLOSSY MOLDING, PANELS PAINTED AN EXACT COLOR MATCH TO THE BOX ARE CRISSCROSSED AND TIED WITH SATINY WHITE RIBBON FOR A FRILLY WAINSCOT TREATMENT. ABOVE, WALLS ARE ONE SHADE LIGHTER. SILKY CURTAIN PANELS WITH RIBBONS WOVEN AND TIED AT THE ENDS COMPLETE THE GIFT-BOX THEME.

SIMPLE SOPHISTICATION

Achieving the beauty of simplicity requires a willingness to pare down. In this living room, barely-there stripes on muted blue walls give way to translucent curtain panels, which are layered to soften the French doors with a whisper of color. A pale palette of eggshell, lavender, periwinkle, celadon, and rose create a serene setting enlivened by the sparkle of silver objects displayed like sculpture on the mantel.

Inspiration...

A SUNNY MORNING ROOM CAPTURES THE LIGHT, EASY FEEL OF THE SEASHORE. PAINTED THE PALEST PERIWINKLE TO REFLECT THE COLORS FOUND INSIDE A SEASHELL, THE ROOM IS REPLETE WITH TOUCHES BORROWED FROM MOTHER NATURE. SEA TURTLES SWIM ON THE CORAL FABRIC ON THE SOFA AND CHAIR. SISAL FLOORING AND RAW LINEN WAINSCOTING BRING TO MIND THE LOOK AND FEEL OF A SANDY SHORELINE. SIMPLE DETAILS EXPRESS THE THEME: A PAINTING OF THE BEACH, WICKER FURNITURE LIKE THAT USED AT OCEANSIDE RESORTS, AND ORNATE SCONCES FASHIONED FROM SEASHELLS. SHEER DRAPERIES TIED TO AN IRON ROD WITH BOWS FILTER THE SUN WITH CASUAL STYLE.

14

IN THE GARDEN A FAVORITE COLLECTIBLE CAN INSPIRE A DECORATING THEME BY SUGGESTING A COLOR SCHEME AS WELL AS SUBJECT MATTER FOR FABRICS AND WALLPAPER. HERE THE COLORS SPRING FROM THE VINTAGE PITCHER, MUG, AND LAMP. YELLOW AND GREEN PLAID LONDON SHADES TAKE THE POTTERY COLORS TO THE WINDOW; A YELLOW FLORAL FABRIC ON THE PILLOW TAKES THE VEGETABLE MOTIF INTO A GENERAL GARDENING THEME AND INTRODUCES THE COMPLEMENTARY NOTE OF PINK THAT BRIGHTENS THE COLOR PALETTE.

RICH RESPLENDENCE THE EXQUISITE BEAUTY OF ANTIQUE FRENCH CHINOISERIE
CANVAS PANELS IS AN OBVIOUS STARTING POINT IN DECORATING THIS FORMAL DINING ROOM. A
CHANDELIER DRIPPING WITH CRYSTALS, CARAMEL-COLOR CURTAINS CAUGHT UP WITH FANCY
TASSELS, AND RICH YELLOW WALLS—ALL COLORS DRAWN FROM THE HUES IN THE PANELS—
EVOKE A WARM, TRADITIONAL SETTING OF GRAND PROPORTIONS.

HIGH AND MIGHTY HIGH CEILINGS OFTEN CAN OVERWHELM A ROOM, PULLING THE EYE AWAY FROM THE INTERIOR'S FOCUS. IN THIS CASE THEIR SOARING HEIGHT IS FLAUNTED, INTEGRATING THE VERTICAL PLANE OF THE ROOM INTO THE DESIGN. RAW SILK CURTAINS IN THE PALEST TAUPE HANG HIGH ABOVE THE TOP OF THE WINDOW FRAME. MONOCHROMATIC HUES ARE CONSISTENT FROM FURNITURE TO WALLS TO CEILING, AND A CHECKERBOARD OF RECTANGLES CAPTURES THE EYE, DRAWING INTEREST UPWARD.

SETTING THE SCENE

Decorating is a discipline, a refinement of design principles that can be used repeatedly from one room to the next. Style, on the other hand, is a matter of taste and preference. Rooms with style reflect an individual passion or personality. The room's essence evolves over time from the homeowner's whims—a new piece is added, accessories are arranged in unusual groupings, and unexpected colors come together accidentally but effectively.

No one can tell you how to infuse style into a room, but there are ways to achieve the mood you want. Begin by choosing the look you most identify with, whether it is eclectic, contemporary, or old-world. Build the bones of your design; then turn to the things you love—your clothes, your garden, your favorite room—to identify your personal style. Experiment and have fun until you arrive at a look that satisfies your soul.

TROPICAL RETREAT THERE IS NO NEED TO LOOK FURTHER THAN AN OCEAN VIEW FOR IDEAS ON DECORATING A SUNROOM. HERE SISAL FLOORING AND WICKER FURNITURE UPHOLSTERED IN SUNWASHED CANVAS CREATE A BEACHY ATMOSPHERE. SIMPLE ROLL-UP SHADES TAKE THE STRIPED FABRIC ON THE SETTEES UP TO CORNICE LEVEL. THE SHADES TIE IN PLACE TO FRAME THE VIEW AND CAN BE UNROLLED FOR PRIVACY AND SHADE.

TRADITIONAL Classic...Timeless...Refined

LUXURIOUS LIVING TRADITIONAL STYLE HAS A RICH REPERTOIRE WITH ROOTS IN THE PAST THAT INFORM ITS PRESENT USE. SUCH IS THE CASE IN THIS COMFORTABLE YET CLASSIC LIVING ROOM, WHERE FURNITURE, ART, AND ACCESSORIES COME TOGETHER WITH FORMAL FLAIR. HAND-PAINTED CANVAS CORNICES INTERPRET A BAROQUE MOTIF WITH A LIGHTHEARTED TOUCH, CROWNING SIMPLE CURTAIN PANELS.

FORMAL FLAIR FULL-LENGTH DRAPERIES WITH FRINGED, PLEATED VALANCES, A POLISHED WALNUT TABLE SURROUNDED BY UPHOLSTERED CHAIRS, AND A BRASS-AND-CRYSTAL CHANDELIER OFTEN ARE FOUND IN FORMAL SETTINGS. IN THIS DINING ROOM THE FORMAL ELEMENTS PARTNER WITH TROPICAL MOTIFS IN THE DRAPERIES AND ON THE WALLS (STENCILED IN SUBTLE GOLDS AND GREENS) IN A NOD TO BRITISH COLONIAL STYLE.

Traditional...

COTTAGE COMFORT

CHECKS AND PRINTS—A TOILE, A VINTAGE-STYLE FRUIT PRINT, A FLORAL STRIPE, AND A STAR-QUILT PILLOW—IN A PALETTE OF MUSTARD, RED, GREEN, AND BLUE DEFINE THIS CORNER WINDOW SEAT AS A COTTAGE-STYLE NOOK. SINCE PRIVACY IS NOT AN ISSUE HERE, THE WINDOWS ARE BARE EXCEPT FOR PLAYFUL VALANCES THAT UNIFY THE ROOM'S CORNER WINDOWS AND COMPLEMENT ITS SUNNY WALLS. IF PRIVACY IS REQUIRED, ROMAN SHADES OR ROLL-UP SHADES CAN BE INSTALLED.

CONTEMPORARY Clean...Simple

OPPOSITES ATTRACT Contemporary style is more than glass, chrome, low furniture, and abstract art. It's spare, clean-lined, and uncluttered and creates drama through high contrast. White walls, ceiling, and window treatments turn traditional architecture into a gallerylike backdrop for modern furnishings and accessories. A scheme of black and white is chic and sophisticated yet welcoming, showing a softer side of contemporary.

CLEAN AND CURRENT AN INVITING SUNROOM DRESSED IN COOL BLUES AND GREENS PUTS TO REST THE NOTION THAT CONTEMPORARY INTERIORS MUST BE COLD AND STARK. ON THE CONTRARY, A TRANQUIL, SPARE ENVIRONMENT IS THE RESULT OF MIXING CLEAN-LINED, DRAMATIC FURNISHINGS IN PALE FABRICS WITH WARM WOODS. FOR A TOUCH OF TEXTURE, THE WALLS ARE LIGHTLY CROSSHATCHED TO REPEAT THE PATTERN FROM THE GAUZY COTTON ROLL-UP SHADES.

RICH NICHE AN EBONY TABLE AND WHITE UPHOLSTERED BENCHES TURN A KITCHEN NOOK INTO AN ELEGANT SPOT FOR MEALS. TO SOFTEN THE FORMAL LOOK, GINGHAM COVERS THE SHADE AND TRIMS THE CURTAINS, AND MATCHING RIBBON CRISSCROSSES PADDED WALLS TO HOLD PHOTOS OF FAMILY VACATIONS. A CURVED EDGE TO THE SHADE OFFERS A SUBTLE COUNTERPOINT TO ALL THE STRAIGHT LINES.

OLD WORLD
Ageless...Understated

RUSTIC ROMANCE OLD-WORLD AMBIENCE AND MODERN CONVENIENCES MELD SEAMLESSLY INTO A STUNNING RE-CREATION OF A 19TH-CENTURY ENGLISH MANOR DINING ROOM AND ENTRY. STRUCTURAL DETAILS SUCH AS PECKY CYPRESS BEAMS AND PANELED WALLS COUPLED WITH CEILINGS SOMETIMES AS LOW AS 7 FEET EVOKE THE LOOK AND FEEL OF A CLASSIC INTERIOR. BUT IT IS THE FRESH, UP-TO-DATE FABRICS FOR THE CURTAINS AND UPHOLSTERY THAT ADD A PUNCH OF PERSONALITY TO THE ROOM.

FRENCH AFFAIR THE GRANDEUR OF AN 18TH-CENTURY FRENCH INTERIOR IS A STUDY IN DECADENT LUXURY, JUST ONE OF MANY STYLES TO EXUDE ROMANCE. A MIRRORED WALL PLAYS UP THE FURNISHINGS, WHICH ARE GILDED AND ORNATE, WHILE HAND-PAINTED DETAILS ARE REPEATED IN THE GOLDEN SWAGS DEPICTED ON THE CROWN MOLDING. THE DRAPERIES, VERTICALLY STRIPED PINK PANELS CROWNED WITH A LUSHLY SWAGGED VALANCE AND JABOT, ARE THE ROOM'S MAIN ATTRACTION.

ROMANTIC Lyrical...Lovely...Dreamy

DEMURE DINING The inviting ambience of a lavender dining room is the result of a few key decisions. First, the color scheme is simple, with lavender and white hues creating a soft contrast throughout. Fabrics are light and billowy, with slipcovers in crushed taffeta and draperies in sheer organza flowing freely to puddle on the floor. Finally, accessories are edited with a disciplined eye, avoiding the excess of period Victorian interiors.

Romantic...

SWEDISH SENSIBILITY Pale pastels, weathered whites, shabby-chic furnishings, and restrained accessorizing are tricks of the trade when mimicking the sweet romance of Swedish style. Light also is essential, with barely-there Roman shades pulled almost out of sight during the day, letting natural light play around the room to cast interesting highlights and shadows.

SWEET DREAMS Tranquillity prevails in this bedroom of soft blue and bright white. A sheer cotton circular canopy creates an ethereal feeling. Loose London shades fit inside the window frame to filter light and allow the wide woodwork to show. Pleated valances cap the shades. Look closely and you'll discover stenciling in the same pale blue painted randomly around the room.

PATTERN PROMENADE

PATTERN IS AN ESSENTIAL PART OF VICTORIAN STYLE, BUT TOO MANY IN A ROOM CAN BE OVERWHELMING. THE STAIR HALL AND DOUBLE PARLOR OF THIS PAINTED LADY FIND A COMFORTABLE BALANCE. PATTERN IS PREVALENT, BUT THE WOODWORK, FURNITURE, AND NEUTRAL-COLOR WALLPAPER OFFSET THE MORE FLAMBOYANT FABRICS AND ORNATE ACCESSORIES.

ANTIQUE INSPIRATION A FLYING-SAUCER LAMPSHADE, WEATHERED BONES AND SEASHELLS, ANTIQUE PARASOLS, A COPPER WEATHER VANE—THESE UNCOMMON OBJECTS BECOME A FEAST FOR THE EYES IN THIS BOLD AND SASSY LIVING ROOM. WHAT MAKES IT WORK? NEUTRAL WALLS AND A FADED ANTIQUE RUG DON'T COMPETE WITH THE FURNITURE AND ACCESSORIES. THE REPETITION OF ONE COLOR—BRILLIANT RED—AND OF SHAPES—RECTANGLES, SQUARES, AND CIRCLES—UNIFIES THE DIVERSITY.

ECLECTIC Collective...Edgy...Interesting

EAST MEETS WEST The fusion of Asian austerity and European sophistication transforms this dining room into an inviting space for convivial entertaining. Many details are traditional with a twist on their presentation. For example, formal drapery panels in mocha, fawn, and pale blue Indian silk grace the windows, while a classic palmetto motif blown up into a 2-foot-tall stencil wraps the room in a subtle band of color.

LESS IS MORE Eclectic doesn't always mean funky. Here rich chocolate walls and crisp white woodwork define a traditional setting worthy of the great interior designer Billy Baldwin. Above the gilt-embellished console, a wood-and-gilt mirror and white scroll brackets bearing urns speak a traditional language. The coffee table and area rug introduce modern accents, as does the dramatic color study hanging above the sofa. The upholstered pieces and simple ceiling-to-floor draperies provide transition between the two contrasting styles.

EXOTIC Seductive...Passionate...Provocative

PASSAGE TO INDIA THIS OPULENT AND DRAMATIC LIVING ROOM SETS THE MOOD FOR MYSTERY. THE KEY? INEXPENSIVE SARIS CUT AND STITCHED INTO COLOR BLOCKS THAT HIGHLIGHT THEIR GOLDEN BANDS AND PAISLEY MOTIFS. THE SECRET OF THE ROOM'S ENERGY IS IN THE CONTRASTS—THE BALANCING OF HEAVY AND LIGHT, OLD AND NEW, STRIPES AND FLORALS. COLOR ALSO CONTRIBUTES TO THE ALLURE. A ZESTY ORANGE HUE IS SPLASHED AROUND THE ROOM ON PILLOWS, CURTAINS, AND THE SOFA SLIPCOVER, CREATING A STRIKING COMPLEMENT TO THE OLIVE GREEN EMBOSSED LINCRUSTA WALLPAPER.

ROOM BY ROOM

3

Who can resist glancing through windows of well-lit houses during a nighttime drive? These glimpses plant seeds for our own future decorating ideas and reaffirm decisions about what we already know we like or don't like.

The same curiosity about how people decorate their spaces is the premise behind this chapter. This collection of images walks you room by room through homes decorated in a variety of styles. This collection emphasizes why certain window and wall treatments are effective, reveals how to coordinate them successfully, and provides pointers on keeping continuity between adjoining rooms without being redundant and boring. Of utmost concern is a room's "liveability." After all, what is the use of having a pretty room if it doesn't work for you and your family?

BUTTERSCOTCH BEAUTY

IN THIS LIVING ROOM, HORIZONTAL AND VERTICAL STRIPES COEXIST, UNIFIED BY BUTTERSCOTCH AND OCHER HUES. THE WALLPAPER STRIPES RUN HORIZONTALLY TO EMPHASIZE THE ROOM'S WIDTH AND DEPTH. ROMAN SHADES INTERRUPT THE FLOW LIKE EXCLAMATION POINTS. SMOCKED AND VELVET-BANDED BURLAP CURTAIN PANELS GIVE THE EYE A PLACE TO PAUSE BETWEEN THE SETS OF STRIPES.

LIVING ROOMS All-Purpose... Comfortable...Restful

WORKING OFF THE CURVE

THE HIGH CONTRAST CREATED BY A NAVY AND WHITE COLOR SCHEME ACCENTUATES THE ARCHITECTURE AND FURNISHINGS IN THIS LIVING ROOM. SUCH STRIKING COLOR PLAY OFTEN NEEDS A COUNTERPOINT TO SOFTEN THE LOOK. WITH ITS SCALLOPED AND RUFFLED EDGES, THE MODIFIED SWAG VALANCE IN TOILE DOES EXACTLY THAT. THE CURVES LOOP ACROSS THE BAY, TRACING A GRACEFUL LINE THAT CONTRASTS WITH THE SHARPLY DEFINED VERTICALS AND HORIZONTALS OF THE WINDOWS. THESE ARE HIGHLIGHTED IN GLOSSY BLACK FRAMED BY WHITE. TO DOWNPLAY THE DARK LINE OF THE BLACK CROWN MOLDING IN THE BAY, A RUFFLED TOP EDGE WAS ADDED TO THE VALANCE. THE FABRIC CARRIES THE EYE TO THE CEILING TO EMPHASIZE THE ROOM'S EXPANSIVE HEIGHT.

BALANCING ACT OPEN FLOOR PLANS ARE VERY POPULAR, BUT DELINEATING ZONES FOR FUNCTION WHILE MAINTAINING FLOW CAN BE DIFFICULT. IN THIS REMODELED KITCHEN AND LIVING ROOM, A LARGE AREA RUG CARVES OUT SPACE FOR THE FAMILY AREA WHILE BARE PLANK FLOORS DEFINE THE KITCHEN. SIMPLE CURTAIN PANELS STITCHED FROM THE SAME FABRIC HANG AT ALL THE WINDOWS, AND A RICH CREAM COLOR ON THE WALLS, CABINETRY, AND CEILING UNIFIES THE TWO SPACES.

Living Rooms...

BERRY BRIGHT THE EASIEST WAY TO CHANGE THE LOOK AND FEEL OF A ROOM IS TO FOCUS ON THE WALLS. THE FULL POTENTIAL OF CORNER WINDOWS IN THIS LIVING ROOM WAS UNREALIZED UNTIL THE ADVENT OF A VIVID RASPBERRY BACKGROUND. SPORTING CUTE HALF-MOON VALANCES AND SHEER PANELS WITH RASPBERRY TAPES TO FILTER LIGHT AND SOFTEN FULL-LENGTH WOODEN BLINDS, THE WINDOWS NOW PLAY A DOMINANT ROLE IN THE DECOR.

SUBTLE SOLUTION ORDINARY FRENCH DOORS WITH A PROMINENT POSITION IN THIS LIVING ROOM BEGGED FOR A PRETTY BUT PRACTICAL TREATMENT. THE SOLUTION? A FABRIC IN THE SAME HUE AS THE WALLS BLENDS WITH THE BACKGROUND, WHILE THE SHAPED CORNICE AND PETAL-POINTED SHADES CREATE A FOCAL POINT. TO KEEP THE DOORS OPERABLE, PULL-DOWN SHADES WERE MOUNTED ON THEM, AND THE FULL-LENGTH DRAPERIES CAN BE PUSHED TO THE SIDES. THE FABRIC CORNICE HIDES THE HARDWARE FOR BOTH.

DINING ROOMS Lively...Intimate...
Opulent...Subdued

RICH REVIVAL THIS DINING ROOM WITH LOW-CONTRAST, TONE-ON-TONE COLORS IS INFUSED WITH INTEREST BY WALLS PLASTERED IN AN OLD-WORLD, MOTTLED FINISH AND A WINDOW DRESSED IN A FORMAL THREE-TIERED TREATMENT. UNEVEN COLOR AND SHEEN ADD DIMENSION TO THE WALLS. THE WINDOW FEATURES A COMPLEX ENSEMBLE: AN UPHOLSTERED CROWN-TOP CORNICE HEIGHTENS THE WINDOW WHILE SWAGS OF LUSH DAMASK SWOOP FROM THE CORNICE AND ACROSS TRIMMED PANELS THAT PUDDLE ON THE FLOOR. THE QUIET COLORS AND HEAVY DETAILING COMBINE WARMTH WITH FORMALITY; THE RESULT IS A SOOTHING PALETTE WITH DEPTH AND STYLE.

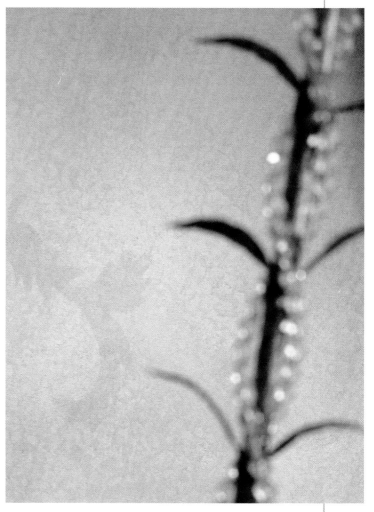

Dining Rooms...

DECORATIVE DECOY FRAMING THE WINDOWS AND FRENCH DOORS WITH MATCHING VALANCES AND FLOOR-LENGTH DRAPERY PANELS UNIFIES THE ROOM SO THAT THE EYE LEAPS OVER THE DIFFERENCES IN THE TWO ARCHITECTURAL ELEMENTS. MOUNTING THE VALANCES JUST BELOW THE CROWN MOLDING MAKES THE CEILING SEEM HIGHER AND MAXIMIZES THE LIGHT AND VIEWS OFFERED BY THE FRENCH DOORS.

QUIET ELEGANCE WALLS UPHOLSTERED IN TAUPE DAMASK AND LUMINOUS FLOOR-TO-CEILING DRAPERIES IN EXQUISITE CHAMPAGNE-COLOR SILK ADD TO THE ENCHANTING GLOW OF THIS FORMAL DINING ROOM. TAPESTRY RIBBON EDGES THE PANELS TO DEFINE THEM; IT ALSO WRAPS THE DRAPERY ROD FOR RICH TEXTURE. IN AN OPULENT INTERPRETATION OF TAB-TOP CURTAINS, THE PANELS HANG FROM WIDE LOOPS KNOTTED WITH FABRIC CHIGNONS. ROMAN SHADES PEEK FROM BEHIND THE PANELS TO ADD PRIVACY AND BLOCK LIGHT.

KITCHENS Functional...Feel-Good... Welcoming...Warm

CONVERGENCE OF CONTRAST COLOR IS CONDUCIVE TO A CHEERFUL KITCHEN. WHITE CABINETRY, COUNTERTOPS, APPLIANCES, AND TRIMWORK EXPAND THIS SPACE AND EMPHASIZE THE ROOM'S CLEAN LINES. CHERRY-RED TROPICAL TOILE WALLPAPER AND VALANCE SPICE UP BRIGHT WHITE WALLS TO MAKE THE ROOM POP. THE RESULTING CONTRAST IS UNMISTAKABLY INVITING AND HOMEY.

Kitchens...

ARTFUL DIVERSION Steer attention away from outdated pickled cabinetry with paint and fabric. An expansive cornice with a shaped edge takes the focus to the ceiling, where stenciled leaves on a sponged background encourage the eye to stay. Crystal pendants along the edge of the cornice catch the light.

BEDROOMS Cozy...Rejuvenating...
Serene...Private

NICE AND EASY THE SECRET TO AN INVITING GUEST ROOM IS A COMFY BED, OF COURSE, BUT AMBIENCE ALSO INDUCES PEACEFUL SLUMBER. FOR A RESTFUL RETREAT, USE A SOFT AND SOOTHING COLOR THROUGHOUT AND INCLUDE ONLY ONE OR TWO BOLD STAND-OUTS IN THE DECOR. HERE, SOFT GREEN FOR PLEATED DRAPERIES, WALLS, FURNITURE, AND BEDDING WRAPS THE ROOM WITH SERENITY. WHITE MOLDING FRAMES HAND-PAINTED MOTIFS TO CREATE SUBTLE DEPTH ON THE WALLS. IN THIS MONOCHROMATIC ENVELOPE, THE BLACK WROUGHT-IRON BED STANDS OUT, PROVIDING NEEDED FOCUS AND PUNCH.

Bedrooms...

SLEEPING IN STYLE Toile with a chinoiserie motif seamlessly envelops a bedroom, creating a cozy, cocoonlike effect. The window treatments, straight curtain panels that overlap, fold back tent-flap-style to reveal plaid lining. Employing allover pattern is a masterful trick that hides flaws in a room and enhances ordinary design features.

PLAYING WITH WALL SPACE HIGH CEILINGS GIVE A SPACE GRANDEUR, BUT THEY ALSO CAN MAKE A ROOM FEEL UNCOMFORTABLY CAVERNOUS. TO LOWER THEM VISUALLY AND GIVE THE ROOM MORE HUMAN-SCALE PROPORTIONS, ADD CROWN MOLDING AND PAINTED BANDS. HERE GOLD STRIPES AND BUTTONS ACCENT THE BANDS. FORMAL SILK DRAPERIES WITH TIGHTLY SMOCKED HEADERS HANG ON GILDED RODS AT THE LEVEL OF THE WINDOW FRAME TO FURTHER SHORTEN THE VERTICAL SPACE.

CHILDREN'S BEDROOMS
Fun...Delightful...
Dreamy...Imaginative

ROOM TO GROW A CHILD'S BED-ROOM POSES A DECORATING CHALLENGE. ON ONE HAND, THE ROOM SHOULD BE OUT-FITTED WITH FURNISHINGS THAT SUIT EACH STAGE OF A CHILD'S DEVELOPMENT. ON THE OTHER, IT SHOULD BE A PERSONABLE SPACE WHERE THE CHILD IS COMFORTABLE AND THE DECOR IS AGE APPROPRIATE. SWEET AND ETHEREAL, THIS NURSERY IS A SOOTHING, RESTFUL PLACE FOR BABY BUT JUST AS EASILY BECOMES A FRILLY RETREAT FOR A YOUNG GIRL.

HARLEQUIN ROMANCE TO DESIGN A ROOM THAT WILL GROW WITH YOUR CHILD, CREATE A TIMELESS FOUNDATION, AVOIDING MOTIFS LIKE CARTOON CHARACTERS THAT WILL DATE THE LOOK. THIS GIRL'S BEDROOM HAS A BASIC COLOR SCHEME OF SALMON AND PINK ENLIVENED BY THE HAND-PAINTED HARLEQUIN DIAMONDS COVERING THE WINDOW-SEAT WALL. A FLOUNCY VALANCE AT THE WINDOW AND HAND-PAINTED SWAGS AROUND THE CEILING LINE ESTABLISH A FORMAL LOOK THAT IS ROMANTIC ENOUGH FOR THE FIT-FOR-A-PRINCESS BED BUT WOULD ALSO WORK FOR A FORMAL AND MORE ADULT DECORATING SCHEME.

BATHROOM BLISS A BATH, HOWEVER SMALL, SHOULD RECEIVE THE SAME CAREFUL ATTENTION AS THE REST OF THE HOUSE. FULL OF PETITE, COZY TOUCHES, THIS ROOM BOASTS FUNCTIONAL TILE WALLS AND A HANDSOME ANTIQUE TUB AND SINK. COVERING THE UPPER WALLS WITH AN ANTIQUE-INSPIRED WALLPAPER AND FRAMING THE NARROW WINDOW WITH A LAVISH SWATH OF SHEER DRAPERY IMBUES THE SPACE WITH UNEXPECTED ELEGANCE.

BATHROOMS Secluded...Blissful... Practical...Stress-Relieving

COMPLEMENTARY CONTRAST MOISTURE, TIGHT SPACE, AND PRACTICALITY MAKE DRESSING A BATHROOM WINDOW PARTICULARLY CHALLENGING. THIS STYLISH BATH WITH DIAMOND-PATTERN WALLPAPER FEATURES ONE WINDOW THAT SERVES AS THE FOCAL POINT. TO PLAY UP ITS DESIGN ASPECTS BUT ALSO PROVIDE PRIVACY AND LIGHT, THE WINDOW TREATMENT PAIRS SHADES AND SHUTTERS. NEAT SHUTTERS MOUNTED INSIDE THE WINDOW FRAME CAN BE CLOSED AT WILL, WHILE A LOOSE BALLOON SHADE THAT MATCHES THE SHOWER CURTAIN EMBELLISHES THE WINDOW WITH LAVISH SOFTNESS.

OUT ON THE PORCH CURTAINS TURN A PORCH INTO AN OPEN-AIR ROOM. THESE HEAVY, WEATHER-RESISTANT CANVAS CURTAINS HANG FROM HOOKS IN THE CEILING AND CAN BE UNTIED AND SPREAD OUT TO HELP BLOCK THE HOT AFTERNOON SUN. IF COMPLETE PRIVACY IS DESIRED, CURTAINS CAN BE HUNG ON CEILING-MOUNTED RODS RUNNING THE LENGTH OF THE PORCH.

BONUS ROOMS Unexpected...
Useful...Beneficial...Creative
...Sunroom

HELLO, SUNSHINE LET LIGHT INTO A SUNROOM WHILE MINIMIZING AN UNAPPEALING VIEW WITH A SWATH OF FABRIC THAT PULLS TO ONE SIDE OF THE WINDOW. A PLEAT AT THE CENTER AND TUCKS AT EACH SIDE GIVE THE PANEL A TAILORED APPEARANCE WHEN IT IS LOWERED. SHROUDING THE FRENCH DOORS WITH FABRIC WOULD CROWD THIS SMALL ROOM, SO THEY ARE LEFT UNDRESSED, AND HOUSEPLANTS PROVIDE A SENSE OF PRIVACY.

Home Office...

TEMPORARY SHADES HOME WORK SPACES MUST BE INVITING—OTHERWISE IT IS EASIER TO RESIST GETTING DOWN TO BUSINESS. HERE AN ARTIST TRIES OUT HIS TEXTILE DESIGNS BY PINNING SAMPLES OVER THE WINDOWS AS GRAPHIC SHADES. SUCH FLAT PANELS LET YOU INTRODUCE AN AFFORDABLE AMOUNT OF LUXURIOUS FABRIC INTO YOUR ROOM.

BONUS POINTS FOR A BONUS ROOM AN ORDINARY SPACE BECOMES THE FAVORITE SPOT IN THE HOUSE, THANKS TO THE UPBEAT, CONTEMPORARY DECOR. A KEY TO THIS ROOM'S SUCCESS IS THE EFFECTIVE USE OF LIGHT FROM THE SMALL DORMER WINDOW. BRIGHT YELLOW STRIPES ON THE WALLPAPER RECALL SUNNY SKIES AND MULTIPLY NATURAL LIGHT, WHILE A SIMPLE VALANCE IN THE SAME WARM HUE DRESSES THE WINDOW WITHOUT BLOCKING ILLUMINATION.

WINDOW
ARCHITECTURE

Windows open a room to the world, drawing in the crucial design element of light—both a functional necessity and a source of interest through highlight and shadow. Windows can frame a view, adding yet another layer to the room's aesthetics, or windows can become art themselves, whether their construction is intricately detailed or simple and spare.

Consider these questions before dressing windows: How can light be channeled into a room without compromising privacy? What is the best way to dress a series of windows along a wall? Are there elegant options for retaining heat in the winter? These and other issues can overwhelm even the most design-savvy homeowner. This chapter presents a collection of windows and complementary treatments that address both the pretty and practical aspects of window dressings.

CURTAIN CALL SUGGESTING THE FORMALITY AND DRAMA OF A THEATER STAGE, THE ANTIQUE VALANCE AND CURTAIN PANELS OF ANTIQUE VOILE SHOWCASE THE ENTIRE RECESSED SPACE OF THIS BAY WINDOW. DRESSING EACH WINDOW INDIVIDUALLY WOULD DETRACT FROM THE VIEW AND INTERFERE WITH THE BUILT-IN SEATING. INSTEAD, THE WINDOW FRAMES AND MUNTINS ARE PAINTED PERIWINKLE BLUE TO CONTRAST WITH THE WALLS AND BRING THE COLORS OF THE GARDEN INSIDE.

ARCHED Graceful...Elegant...Old-World

REGAL RESTRAINT If only every window could have the architectural appeal of an arch or curve. In this bedroom custom iron rods that conform to the curve of the window are mounted outside the arch, allowing cotton sheers to cascade in graceful folds over the entire window.

BEAUTY IN THE BATH THE MOST POPULAR WAY OF DRESSING AN ARCHED WINDOW IS TO HANG CURTAINS HALFWAY UP, LEAVING THE ARCH EXPOSED. IN THIS BATH, WITH ITS EXPANSIVE RURAL VIEWS, ORDINARY CAFE CURTAINS ON IRON RINGS HANG FROM AN IRON ROD THAT MATCHES THE IRON WINDOW FRAME, PROVIDING PRIVACY WHEN NEEDED.

GOTHIC
Architectural...
Ornate...Dramatic

INCURABLE ROMANTIC

A WINDOW TREATMENT WOULD DETRACT FROM THIS GOTHIC-STYLE ATTIC WINDOW. INSTEAD, PAINTING THE SURROUNDING WALL DANDELION YELLOW ACCENTUATES THE DISTINCTIVE SHAPE. IN KEEPING WITH THE COTTAGE STYLE OF THE ROOM, COLLECTIBLE PLATES FURTHER EMPHASIZE THE LINES.

ARCHITECTURE AS ART WHEN A WINDOW OR DOOR BOASTS BEAUTIFUL ARCHITECTURAL DETAILS, A MINIMAL TREATMENT—OR NONE AT ALL, AS IN THIS ROOM (OPPOSITE)—IS THE BEST DESIGN OPTION. IF YOU MUST COVER THE SPACE TO PROCURE PRIVACY, CHOOSE PANELS THAT BLEND INCONSPICUOUSLY INTO THE WALLS AND THAT CAN BE DRAWN COMPLETELY TO THE SIDES TO ALLOW THE DOOR TO OPERATE EASILY.

DARINGLY DIFFERENT FRENCH DOORS FLANKED BY WINDOWS MIMIC THE LOOK OF A BAY WINDOW BUT NEED A TREATMENT THAT ALLOWS THE DOORS TO OPEN WITHOUT CONSTRAINT. THE SOLUTION WAS TO EMPLOY TWO TREATMENTS: BALLOON VALANCES FOR THE SIDE WINDOWS AND FULL-LENGTH CURTAIN PANELS THAT SLIDE TO THE SIDES FOR THE FRENCH DOORS. CONTINUITY BETWEEN THE TWO DESIGNS IS ACHIEVED BY USING THE SAME FABRIC AND A CUSTOM ROD THAT BENDS AT THE CORNERS.

BAY WINDOWS Curvy...Romantic...Extravagant

SHEER SERENITY ROMAN SHADES, FABRICATED FROM SHEER EMBROIDERED LINEN VOILE, HINT AT PART BOUDOIR, PART GARDEN ROOM, AND PART SPA IN THIS MASTER BATH. THEIR SIMPLE CONSTRUCTION AND DEMURE FLORAL MOTIF ARE A BEAUTIFUL BALANCE TO THE INTRICATE MOLDINGS ON THE BAY WINDOW AND ORNATE TILEWORK IN THE BATH.

CURVE APPEAL FLORAL VALANCES LAYERED OVER SOLID GATHERED UNDERSKIRTS CALL ATTENTION TO THIS ROOM'S LOFTY HEIGHT. IVORY LACE CAFE CURTAINS HUNG AT THE HALFWAY POINT PROVIDE PRIVACY WITHOUT BLOCKING SUNLIGHT OR THE OUTSIDE VIEW.

PICTURE WINDOW Scenic...Expansive

SHUTTERED FOR STYLE THE POINT OF A PICTURE WINDOW IS TO WELCOME THE OUTDOORS INSIDE, SO WHY HIDE IT WITH DRAPERIES? HANGING OLD SHUTTERS ON EACH SIDE OF THE WINDOW FRAME REINFORCES THE ILLUSION OF DISSOLVING THE BOUNDARIES BETWEEN INSIDE AND OUT. THE SHUTTERS ARE DECORATIVE RATHER THAN FUNCTIONAL AND SOFTEN THE MODERN LOOK OF THE WINDOW WITH EUROPEAN STYLE.

PANELED PRESENCE ALTHOUGH PICTURE WINDOWS ARE USUALLY SINGLE LARGE PANES OF GLASS, FIXED MULTIPANED WINDOWS ALSO FALL INTO THIS CATEGORY. OPTING FOR PAINT RATHER THAN FABRIC FOR THE WINDOW TREATMENT EMPHASIZES THE WINDOWS AS AN ARCHITECTURAL FEATURE IN THIS SITTING ROOM. BLACK FRAMES AND MUNTINS SET INTO WHITE WALLS SPOTLIGHT THE WINDOWS AS FOCAL POINTS AND GIVE THE ROOM A CLEAN, MODERN LOOK.

SASHES Popular...Hard-Working...Versatile

BALANCED BLEND MULTIPANE, DOUBLE-HUNG WINDOWS ARE HALLMARKS OF 18TH-CENTURY ARCHITECTURE AND TRADITIONALLY WERE PAINTED WHITE TO STAND OUT FROM THE WALLS. IF YOU PREFER TO CREATE A CONTINUOUS ENVELOPE OF COLOR, PAINT THEM TO BLEND IN WITH THE WALLS. IN THIS LIVING ROOM, THE WOODWORK RECEDES SO THE EYE FOCUSES ON THE FURNISHINGS AND ART INSTEAD OF THE ARCHITECTURE.

SWEET DECEIT SASH WINDOWS EASILY CAN BE DRESSED UP TO RESEMBLE A MORE DECORATIVE ARCH. THE SECRET LIES IN THE WINDOW TREATMENT. A CURVED, UPHOLSTERED CORNICE CUT GENEROUSLY PAST THE SIDES OF THE WINDOW IS PAIRED WITH FULL-LENGTH DRAPERIES, BOTH OF WHICH ARE TRIMMED IN SILK TASSELS TO TIE THE LOOK TOGETHER.

Sashes...

SUPREMELY SUBDUED AN OVERSIZE BEDROOM IS GRACED WITH A SERIES OF WINDOWS ALONG ONE WALL, BOTH A WELCOME LUXURY AND A DESIGN CHALLENGE. FULL-LENGTH CURTAIN PANELS COLOR-COORDINATED WITH THE WALLS HANG ON EXPOSED METAL RODS AND PUDDLE ON THE FLOOR—A GOOD CHOICE FOR AN INTERIOR THAT COULD BE OVER-POWERED BY A MULTIPLICITY OF HEAVY WINDOW TREATMENTS.

CASEMENTS Clean...Classic...Traditional...Airy

TAILORED TASTE INSTEAD OF DRESSING NARROW CASEMENTS INDIVIDUALLY, WHICH CREATES A SPOTTY EFFECT, PULL THEM TOGETHER WITH AN OVERSIZE SWAG VALANCE. INSTALLED AT THE CEILING LINE, THE TREATMENT SOFTENS THE RECTANGULAR SHAPES OF THE WINDOWS AND "WIDENS" THEIR PROPORTIONS.

CHECKMATE OLDER HOMES OFTEN FEATURE CASEMENT WINDOWS ALONG THE UPPER SECTION OF WALLS. TO LENGTHEN THESE WINDOWS AND PROVIDE A COLORFUL BACKDROP TO THE BEDS, FULL-LENGTH DRAPERY PANELS IN A SMART COTTON CHECK HANG OVER THE WINDOWS AND EXTEND AROUND THE CORNER TO THE OTHER WALLS IN THE ROOM.

A CUBBY WITH CHARISMA Two single-pane casement windows shed the only light in this attic room. Rather than cover the available light with curtains, the designer topped the casements with a tailored cornice. A simple half-circle swag of checked sheer silk softens the architecture.

ARTFUL EDITING FUSSY CURTAINS WOULD SEEM OUT OF PLACE ON THIS CASUAL SUN-
PORCH, PLUS THEY WOULD BLOCK THE VIEW AND THE LIGHT. THE FRAMES, THEREFORE, WERE
PAINTED AN UNOBTRUSIVE GRAY THAT ADDS DEMURE DEFINITION AND KEEPS THE WINDOWS
FROM FADING INTO THE FRAMES.

SWEET SUBTLETY NEUTRAL IN TONE, THESE FLOOR-TO-CEILING DRAPERY PANELS MIX AND MATCH WITH THE MONOCHROMATIC COLOR SCHEME AND ADD HEIGHT TO THE ROOM. THE OVERSCALE CHECKERBOARD PATTERN IS SHEER FABRIC THAT ALLOWS LAYERS OF IVORY AND GREEN TO SHIMMER THROUGH EACH OTHER.

LUMINOUS LOOK WALL-TO-WALL WINDOWS ARE THE CENTER OF ATTENTION IN THIS BREAKFAST ROOM CARVED OUT OF A KITCHEN CORNER. A SASSY VALANCE LEAVES THE REPETITIVENESS OF GRIDDED MUNTINS EXPOSED, ALLOWING SUNSHINE TO FLOW FREELY INTO THE BREAKFAST ROOM AND PREVENTING THE HEAVILY WOODED SCENERY FROM BEING OBSCURED.

SENSATIONAL STYLE

At the very least, a room must meet the essentials of basic shelter: windows for light and walls and a roof for blocking the elements. After function, however, it's the senses that dictate style: the feel of cool, smooth marble underfoot; a slant of light highlighting the coarseness of Venetian plastered walls; the caress of a cashmere throw; a crackling fire and its dancing shadows. Together, three-dimensional layers achieve a chemistry that tantalizes and conveys comfort—the essence of good design to which professionals aspire.

Walls and windows become focal points in rooms where the senses are stimulated through color, contrast, texture, and pattern. Indeed, one of the oldest tricks of the trade is learning how these elements relate to each other and their surroundings. Too much of one and not enough of another can lead to unfortunate results, but what sweet harmony when a delicate balance is struck.

ORANGE CRUSH HOW DO YOU KNOW WHEN A COLOR PLAN IS EFFECTIVE? WHEN IT GARNERS AN EMOTIONAL RESPONSE, SUCH AS THE UPLIFTING, CHEERY FEEL EVOKED BY THIS SITTING ROOM. ORANGE, GREEN, AND PURPLE ARE SPACED EQUALLY ON THE COLOR WHEEL, FORMING A TRIADIC SCHEME—A KEY TO THE ROOM'S BALANCE AND HARMONY.

COLOR Sizzle...Soothe...Enliven...Delight

COLOR PLAN WITH PIZZAZZ

COLOR MAKES A ROOM SING. OF ALL DESIGN ELEMENTS, NO OTHER EXPRESSES PERSONALITY, AFFECTS MOOD, AND TRANSFORMS A ROOM AS EASILY AS COLOR. YET IT REMAINS THE MOST DAUNTING OF DECORATING CHOICES, OFTEN PARALYZING HOMEOWNERS INTO PLAYING IT SAFE WITH TRIED-AND-TRUE NEUTRALS. USING A COLOR WHEEL (AVAILABLE AT ART SUPPLY STORES AND PAINT STORES) CAN HELP YOU BREAK OUT OF THAT BOX BY SHOWING YOU HOW COLORS RELATE TO ONE ANOTHER. PURPLE, LIME GREEN, AND ORANGE ENLIVEN THIS DINING ROOM WITH A CELEBRATION OF HUES THAT, WHEN USED TOGETHER, MAKE EACH POP WITH PERSONALITY. GREEN AND PURPLE SHARE A COMMON "PARENT COLOR" OF BLUE AND ARE COOL HUES. ORANGE SHARES A YELLOW UNDERTONE WITH GREEN BUT IS A WARM COLOR. SATISFYING COLOR SCHEMES ACHIEVE A BALANCE BETWEEN WARM AND COOL TONES BY DRAWING FROM OPPOSITE SIDES OF THE COLOR WHEEL OR BY CHOOSING RELATED COLORS THAT RANGE FROM WARM TO COOL.

Color...

THINK PINK Custom floor-to-ceiling silk curtain panels with pink peeking out from the folds serve as the ideal backdrop for this vintage Hollywood-style guest suite. The room is furnished with contemporary and vintage pieces. Hot pink pops out from throw pillows, framed art, even book dust jackets, providing contrast and tying the room together.

A SPLASH OF CITRUS Bold lime green walls infuse this teen art studio with energy. Sheer checked panels hung from the ceiling screen two end windows to soften the architecture and emphasize the room's generous and airy height.

Color...

SERENELY GREEN Multiple shades of green mimic the peaceful, soothing effects of nature. Mixing different hues of the same color produces a monochromatic scheme. Variety and interest come from the mix of patterns and solids. A white ceiling, bedspread, and accessories offer visual relief.

WINSOME WONDERLAND WHITE IS ONE OF THE FEW COLORS THAT IS SUCCESSFUL TIME AND AGAIN IN A TONE-ON-TONE DECORATING SCHEME. THIS RESTFUL RETREAT IS THE RESULT OF SUBTLE VARIATIONS OF WHITE COMBINED WITH THE TEXTURAL APPEAL OF A CANVAS SHADE, SHEER ORGANDY BED CANOPY AND SKIRT, AND COTTON WINDOW PANELS.

CREATING CALM NEVER WAKE A SLEEPING BABY—IT IS A RULE OF PARENTHOOD THAT REMAINS UNCOMPROMISED IN THIS ALL-WHITE NURSERY. ALMOST EVERY DESIGN ELEMENT IN THE ROOM, FROM THE CHENILLE CURTAINS TO THE PAINTED WALLS, IS A CREAMY WHITE THAT CREATES A PEACEFUL, RESTFUL ATMOSPHERE. A BIRCH TREE BRANCH WRAPPED WITH NATURAL GRAPEVINE INTRODUCES UNEXPECTED TEXTURE AS A CURTAIN ROD. NATURAL WICKER ANCHORS THE ETHEREAL ROOM WITH A COLOR BLOCK OF WARM BROWN.

Color...

ASTOUNDING BROWN THE
WALL-TO-WALL WARMTH OF DARK RED
GIVES THIS LIBRARY A COZY, DENLIKE FEEL.
RAW UMBER UPHOLSTERY, SILK TONE-ON-
TONE DRAPERIES, AND THE BOOKCASE
WALL ARE SIMILAR IN TONE TO THE WALLS
AND LEATHER-TRIMMED BOOKCASE
SHELVES AND SUPPORTS. THIS PRESERVES
THE LOW-CONTRAST HARMONY OF THE
SPACE. THE GILDED CHAIR AND BRASS
STUDS CATCH THE LIGHT TO ADD NEEDED
SPARKLE.

NEUTRAL TERRITORY A NEUTRAL COLOR SCHEME DEPENDS ON DIVERSITY OF TEXTURES TO PROVIDE INTEREST. HERE, BAMBOO SHADES, POLISHED WOOD BED POSTS, A SMOOTH LEATHER CHAIR, A GILDED WOOD TABLE, A WOOL CARPET, A CHENILLE THROW, AND A TAPESTRY FOOTSTOOL OFFER A PALETTE OF TOUCHABLE TEXTURES. IN ADDITION, THE DARK WOOD OF THE BED AND DRAPERY RODS, BLACK LEATHER CHAIR, AND BLACK LAMPSHADE GROUND THE ROOM AND GIVE THE NEUTRAL SCHEME DEPTH.

DARK AND DRAMATIC AGAINST CHARCOAL WALLS AND WHITE WAINSCOTING, A BLACK-AND-GOLD STRIPED ZIGZAG VALANCE AND GOLDEN SILK PANELS MAKE THIS WINDOW A FOCAL POINT. REPEATING THE GOLD NOTE IN THE UPHOLSTERY CREATES UNITY.

SUN-KISSED CHARISMA THE MORE CONTINUOUS A COLOR IS IN A SPACE, THE
LARGER THE SPACE LOOKS AND FEELS. IN THIS TINY KITCHEN, SHADES OF SUNNY YELLOW
UNIFY THE CABINETRY, TILES, WINDOW TREATMENT, CROWN MOLDING, AND DIAMOND-PATTERN
WALLPAPER. THE FLOW OF COLOR KEEPS THE EYE MOVING, CREATING THE IMPRESSION THAT
THE SPACE IS LARGER THAN IT REALLY IS.

110

YEARNING FOR YELLOW NATURAL LIGHT THAT DANCES INTO THIS LIVING ROOM IS AN ASSET WELL WORTH CAPITALIZING UPON. BOLD COLOR WOULD BE ONE WAY TO BRIGHTEN THE SPACE, BUT A NEUTRAL COLOR SCHEME WITH SOFT BUTTERY YELLOW ACCENTS OFFERS A LIGHT-ENHANCING AND SOPHISTICATED ALTERNATIVE. THE WINDOWS ARE FRAMED WITH SWATHS OF CRUSHED SILK, JUST ENOUGH FABRIC TO MAKE A STATEMENT WITHOUT KEEPING THE LIGHT FROM SHINING THROUGH.

MOODY BLUE IF PAINTING AN ENTIRE ROOM IN COLONIAL BLUE SEEMS LIKE TOO GREAT A RISK—TOO OVERWHELMING—REMEMBER THAT LARGE DOSES OF WHITE OR EVEN GRAY WILL PROVIDE VISUAL RELIEF. RICH BROWN WOODS AND GOLD-TONE ACCENTS PROVIDE A WARM COUNTERPOINT TO THE COOL BLUE, GIVING THIS ROOM QUIET ELEGANCE.

PATCHWORK PRESENCE WHO WOULDN'T WANT TO CURL UP WITH A GOOD BOOK IN THIS COZY WINDOW SEAT? THE RUSTIC RED, WARM YELLOW, AND DENIM BLUE DEFINITELY PLAY A PART IN SETTING THE SCENE, BUT IT IS THE MIX OF PATTERNS —THE UP-TO-DATE PATCHWORK SHADE, TOILE SEAT CUSHION, FRINGED PILLOWS, STRIATED WOODWORK, AND TEXTURED WALLS—THAT TAKE THE LEAD IN ELICITING CASUAL COMFORT.

THREE-PART HARMONY A TOILE, A LARGE-SCALE PRINT, AND THREE VARIETIES OF LACE EASILY COULD OVERPOWER THIS FRENCH BOUDOIR. YET A COLOR SCHEME (INSPIRED BY THE AUBUSSON CARPET) OF BROWN AND RED LIGHTENED WITH PLENTY OF CREAM LENDS BALANCE AND KEEPS A MIXTURE OF DISPARATE PATTERNS FROM BECOMING CHAOTIC.

Pattern...

BOLD BEAUTY A MIX OF FABRIC
PATTERNS IN LIVELY SHADES OF RED,
YELLOW, AND GREEN MAKES A STRONG
STATEMENT FOR PERSONAL STYLE.
BRICK RED REPEATS THROUGHOUT
THE ROOM, APPEARING IN WALLPAPER,
CUSHIONS, AND ROMAN SHADES.
LARGE AREAS OF SOLID COLOR—IN THE
SOFA AND A COLUMN OF DRAPERY
THAT FUNCTIONS AS A PORTIERE—PRO-
VIDE VISUAL RELIEF AND ANCHOR THE
PALETTE OF PATTERNS. MOROCCAN
TABLES ADD YET MORE PATTERN WITH
THEIR INLAID DECORATION.

...Pattern

PERFECT POISE Color is the key to blending a variety of patterns in a room. In this den, which doubles as a guest room, patterns include a large-scale multicolor scenic print at the windows, wallpaper that recalls damask, a flower-strewn rug, a tone-on-tone geometric on the club chair, and subtle men's suiting plaid on the sofa. Threads of rust, ocher, and taupe tie them all together for understated harmony.

...Pattern

TOILE RETREAT WITH A SLANTED CEILING AND ONE WINDOW, THIS 8x13-FOOT PETITE GUEST ROOM IN A SEASIDE COTTAGE POSED MORE CHALLENGE THAN CHARM. TO DOWNPLAY ITS SMALL SIZE AND ODD SHAPE, A SIMPLE TOILE PATTERN FEATURING SEASHELLS WAS WRAPPED AROUND THE WALLS AND WINDOW. INDEED, HOMEOWNERS HESITANT TO USE A SINGLE PATTERN REPETITIOUSLY SHOULD CONSIDER TOILE, AS IT IS ONE OF THE EASIER PATTERNS TO MASTER WITH SUCCESS.

Pattern...

CHILD'S PLAY WITH SO MANY FUN
CHOICES FOR WALLPAPER, BEDDING, AND
ACCESSORIES, DECORATING A CHILD'S
ROOM IS AN ADVENTURE IN CREATIVITY. AN
OBVIOUS OPTION IS TO INCORPORATE
DELIGHTFUL PATTERNS THAT VISUALLY
REPRESENT THE FANTASY, ENERGY, AND
MOVEMENT ASSOCIATED WITH CHILDHOOD.
HERE FLORALS AND DIAMONDS STIMULATE
THE IMAGINATION WITHOUT OVERPOWER-
ING A CHILD'S SLEEPING SPACE.

SHIMMER AND SHINE TEXTURE IS WHAT GIVES DECOR THAT EXTRA OOMPH. IT MAY WELL BE THE MOST SUBTLE OF DESIGN ELEMENTS, BUT ITS EFFECT CAN BE POTENT. FOR STARTERS, TEXTURE INVITES A NEW SENSE INTO DESIGN—THAT OF TOUCH. WHILE THE PRESENCE OF COLOR AND PATTERN IS EVIDENT THE INSTANT YOU WALK INTO A ROOM, TEXTURE REQUIRES EXPLORATION AND AN EYE FOR DETAIL. TEXTURE ALSO PROVIDES PSYCHOLOGICAL DEPTH AND TRUE DIMENSION, ADDING COMPLEXITY TO THE COMPOSITION OF A ROOM. ROUGH TEXTURES ABSORB COLOR AND ARE VIEWED AS MORE CASUAL AND UNDERSTATED. SMOOTH, SHINY TEXTURES LIKE THOSE IN THIS LIVING ROOM ARE FORMAL AND REFLECTIVE, ADDING EXCITEMENT TO A TONE-ON-TONE DESIGN. A TABLE SKIRT IN MINTY METALLIC TAFFETA, SHIMMERY CURTAIN PANELS OF GOLDEN SATIN, AND SILKY WALLPAPER IN AQUA STRIPES ARE ELEGANT CHOICES FOR A SINGLE-TONE SETTING.

GENTLE NUANCE THE NEUTRAL COLOR SCHEME OF BLACK AND BEIGE RELIES ON THE TEXTURES IN THE ROOM FOR INTEREST. BAMBOO-PRINT WALLPAPER, A RATTAN SIDE TABLE, AND A BURLAP ROMAN SHADE ADD DIMENSION TO THE CASUAL DECOR.

GENTEEL TRADITION A DECORATING STATEMENT DOESN'T HAVE TO SCREAM WITH COLOR AND CONTRAST TO MAKE ITS POINT. RATHER, SOME OF THE MOST SUCCESSFUL VIGNETTES ARE SUBTLE AND SUGGESTIVE, AS SHOWN ON THIS STAIRCASE LANDING. TEXTURE FROM POLISHED WOOD, A BILLOWY BALLOON SHADE, A DIAMOND-PANE WINDOW, AND WARM YELLOW WALLS WITH HAND-PAINTED STENCILS TRANSFORM A SMALL AND USUALLY UNDECORATED SPOT INTO THE FOCAL POINT OF A TRANSITIONAL SPACE.

Texture...

LOVELY LINEN AN ELEGANT DISGUISE, THE MOTTLED FLORAL MOTIF ON THESE WALLS APPEARS TO BE ANTIQUE WALLPAPER BUT IS ACTUALLY WOVEN LINEN STRETCHED FROM FLOOR TO CEILING. WHEN COMBINED WITH DAMASK, RAW SILK, VELVET, AND EGYPTIAN COTTON ELSEWHERE IN THE ROOM, THE LAVISH WALLCOVERING MAKES GUESTS FEEL AS THOUGH THEY HAVE LANDED IN THE LAP OF LUXURY.

PEEK AT CHIC French furnishings, high ceilings, and faux-paneled walls evoke a Parisian apartment. The mottled walls mimic aged plaster, while a draped swag and jabot layered over silk curtain panels soften the faux texture and lend height and drama to the room.

Texture...

REFINED DESIGN SPARE AND
SLEEK, A MODERN LIVING ROOM CARVED
OUT OF A CORNER IN A ONE-LEVEL LOFT
RELIES ON TEXTURE FOR DEPTH AND
INTEREST. IN THIS HIGHLY EDITED ROOM,
ROUGH, PAINTED BRICK WALLS CONTRAST
WITH THE SMOOTH SURFACES OF GLOSSY
WOOD FURNITURE, POLISHED CONCRETE
FLOORS, LEATHER CHAIRS, AND INDUSTRI-
AL METAL WINDOWS.

Texture...

ON THE SURFACE TEXTURE CAN BE VISUAL AS WELL AS TACTILE. RAISED MOLDINGS APPLIED TO WALLS AND CARVED ANTIQUE SCREENS DOUBLING AS DOORS INVITE YOU TO RUN YOUR HAND OVER THE SURFACES TO FEEL THEIR DEPTH AND DIMENSION. ON THE WINDOWS INEXPENSIVE MATCHSTICK BLINDS INTRODUCE A COARSE TEXTURE THAT CONTRASTS WITH POLISHED WOOD AND SMOOTH UPHOLSTERY.

IN TOUCH WITH THE TROPICS WOVEN GRASS PANELS FRAMED WITH STRIPS OF LATH BRING SHIMMERING TEXTURE TO THE WALLS OF THIS DINING ROOM. AN UNLIKELY LEAD DESIGN ELEMENT, THE WOVEN TEXTURE CAPTURES THE FEEL OF BRITISH COLONIAL ARCHITECTURE WHILE SERVING AS A SUBTLE ASIAN-INSPIRED BACKDROP FOR A COLLECTION OF EASTERN ART AND ANTIQUES.

CONTRAST Artful...Interesting... Paradoxical...Unexpected

BROWN AND WHITE LIGHT AND DARK. SMOOTH AND ROUGH. WARM AND COOL. SOLID AND PATTERNED. CONTRAST IS SIMPLY THE JUXTAPOSITION OF DISSIMILAR ELEMENTS, AND IT IS THAT FRICTION THAT ACTUALLY BRINGS THESE ELEMENTS TOGETHER TO INVIGORATE AND ADD VERVE TO A ROOM. LIKE PATTERN, CONTRAST WORKS BEST WHEN A COMMONALITY EXISTS, WHETHER IT IS TEXTURE, IMAGERY, OR REPETITION. IN THIS BEDROOM, HORIZONTAL STRIPES ON THE WALL IN SHINY AND FLAT SHEENS OFFER A SUBTLE CONTRAST, WHILE THE HEADBOARD AND DRAPERIES STAND OUT BOLDLY. THE CHOCOLATE AND CREAM WINDOWPANE-CHECK DRAPERIES HANG FROM BROWN FINIALS THAT POP CRISPLY AGAINST THE WALLS. CONTRASTS IN LINE AND TEXTURE ACCENTUATE THE DESIGN: A CURVACEOUS LAMP AND HALF-ROUND DRUM TABLE FLANK A RECTANGULAR HEADBOARD, AND THE BED, WITH ITS TAILORED COVERLET AND SKIRT, IS SOFT-ENED BY A FAUX FUR BOLSTER AND BUMPY CHENILLE THROW.

Contrast...

DECIDEDLY DIFFERENT THE MENU FOR SUCCESS IN AN ALL-NEUTRAL DINING ROOM RELIES ON THE ELEMENT OF CONTRAST. ROUGH-HEWN TONGUE-AND-GROOVE FIR CEILINGS CLEARLY CONVEY AN ARTS AND CRAFTS INFLUENCE, BUT THE TUFTED CORNICES IN NUBBY COTTON ARE TAILORED AND SOPHISTICATED, MODERNIZING THE ROOM. THE REPETITION OF SQUARES—IN RECTANGULAR WINDOWPANES, UPHOLSTERED SQUARES ON THE CORNICE, AND THE DIAMOND PATTERN ON THE CHAIRS—CREATES A PLEASING RHYTHM, WITH A ROUND TABLE INSERTING THE CONTRASTING NOTE.

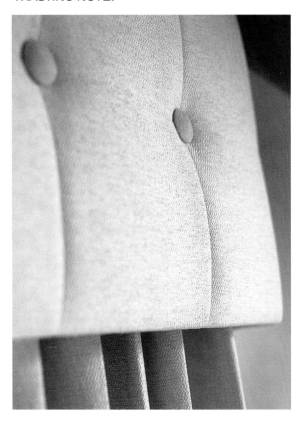

Contrast...

QUIET BACKGROUND White walls and oatmeal-color valances create a light-filled, low-key environment in this sitting room and focus attention on the furnishings. These furnishings introduce the contrasts that give the room personality: casual wicker alongside formal ebony and walnut woods and dressy damask partnered with a cottage check and exotic zebra print.

FILTERED FRAMEWORK THE WEIGHTINESS OF THE UPHOLSTERY AND RUG MIGHT LEAD YOU TO EXPECT HEAVY DRAPERIES AT THE WINDOWS. INSTEAD, SHEER ORGANDY PANELS FRAME AND SOFTEN THE ROOM AND EMPHASIZE THE GENEROUS WINDOWS.

...Contrast

KITCHEN CONFIDENCE IN THIS
CLASSIC KITCHEN. YELLOW WALLS, WHITE
WOODWORK, AND A BLUE CEILING INVOKE
A CLASSIC COLOR SCHEME. INSTEAD OF
THE PREDICTABLE BLUE ACCENTS, HOW-
EVER, TOUCHES OF BLACK AND GRAY
ACCENT THE SCHEME FOR A SOPHISTICAT-
ED LOOK. THE SPECKLED GRANITE COUN-
TERTOP IS THE INSPIRATION, AND HAND-
PAINTED LAMBREQUINS AND BLACK
MENSWEAR PLAID TRIM ON THE CURTAINS
CARRY OUT THE THEME.

Contrast...

PATTERN PLAY Contrasting patterns add interest to a room. Here the geometry of a checked bed skirt and curtain panels plays against an organic tone-on-tone leaf-print wallpaper. A floral rug asserts a stronger floral personality, but the room's overall style is tailored. Note the coral stripe running through the plaid fabric—it's the same color as the walls and the flowers in the rug.

STYLE STATEMENT Transitions between different spaces in your home hardly have to be bland. In this traditional-style home, a khaki striped wallpaper and teal plaid window shade on the staircase landing set up a dialogue of contrasting pattern and color to give the spot quiet charm.

WELL-DRESSED
WINDOWS

How do you decide which type of treatment will work best for your window and reflect your personal flair? A starting point is to use the style of your window as a guide. A window with shapely, attractive architecture is an asset to be accentuated by its treatment. A basic window, on the other hand, allows an imaginative and creative treatment to change the way a room looks and feels. If shape differs from one window to the next in the same room, use the same fabric and the same or similar treatments on all windows to unify the decor.

Another option is to consider the style of the room. Contemporary interiors generally have streamlined window treatments, while more traditional spaces are likely to have full-length draperies and cornices. Remember that form follows function: A treatment must allow the operation of the window, with aesthetics a close second on the list of priorities.

PARISIAN RETREAT PINCH-PLEAT DRAPERIES ARE THE SAME HUE AS THE WALLS, MAINTAINING VISUAL UNITY IN THIS BEDROOM. SHEER PANELS DIFFUSE THE SUNSHINE AND SOFTEN THE LIGHT. FLORAL TRIM EDGING THE PANELS IS AN UNEXPECTED, PLAYFUL TOUCH IN AN OTHERWISE SOPHISTICATED ROOM.

Versatile...Comfortable

LONG AND LUSH A SCREEN THAT CAN BE DRAWN BACK OR UP—THIS IS THE MOST BASIC DEFINITION OF A CURTAIN, BUT IT FALLS SHORT OF CAPTURING THE ATTRACTIVE ATTRIBUTES OF THIS UTILITARIAN DESIGN ELEMENT. (NOTE THAT "DRAPERY" IS DEFINED AS HEAVY FABRIC USED AS A CURTAIN; DRAPERY USUALLY IMPLIES FORMALITY AND A FLOOR-LENGTH TREATMENT WHILE "CURTAIN" IS OFTEN USED TO DESCRIBE SHORT OR INFORMAL TREATMENTS.) THIS DINING ROOM FEATURES A WINDOW TREATMENT AS GLAMOROUS AS AN EVENING GOWN. LONG PINCH-PLEAT DRAPERIES OF CELADON GREEN AND CREAMY WHITE STRIPES HANG JUST BELOW THE CROWN MOLDING AND SWEEP THE FLOOR, DESCRIBING AN ELEGANT VERTICAL THAT RAISES THE APPARENT HEIGHT OF THE CEILING. LONG, FULL DRAPERIES LEND FORMALITY TO A ROOM. TO GIVE PANELS THE BODY TO STAND OUT FROM THE WALL LIKE THIS, DESIGNERS RECOMMEND USING STIFF INTERLINING AS WELL AS LINING.

Draperies & Curtains...

FORMALITY WITH FLOUNCE

PATTERNED DRAPERY PANELS WITH A CHERRY RED GROUND AND COORDINATING CAMEL-COLOR SHADES GIVE AN AIR OF FORMALITY TO A LIVELY KITCHEN WITH FAUX-GRASS-CLOTH WALLS. A CAMEL-COLOR BAND TRIMS THE DRAPERY PANELS FOR EMPHASIS. THE CLASSIC PRINT AND THE DRESSMAKER DETAIL OF WIDE, SMOCKED HEADINGS ADD POLISH TO THE PRESENTATION. BRAIDED TIEBACKS WRAPPED HIGH AROUND THE PANELS CORRAL THE DRAPERIES SO THEY DO NOT BLOCK VIEWS.

Draperies & Curtains...

A LESSON IN LACE PANELS OF SHEER LACE HIGHLIGHT RATHER THAN HIDE THE DIFFERENT WINDOWS IN A SPANISH COLONIAL REVIVAL LIVING ROOM. THE ARCHED WINDOW IS A HALLMARK OF THIS CLASSIC STYLE, AND THE CAFE CURTAINS POSITIONED HALFWAY DOWN SCREEN FOR PRIVACY WITHOUT COVERING ITS BEAUTY. ON THE CASEMENT WINDOWS FULL-LENGTH PANELS HANG TO THE FLOOR JUST AS THE CAFE CURTAINS DO, ILLUSTRATING THE LESSON OF USING THE SAME FABRICS AND SIMILAR TREATMENTS TO UNIFY DIFFERENT WINDOW STYLES. A SWAGGED VALANCE CREATES A PLEASING COUNTERPOINT TO THE ARCHED WINDOW.

ENVELOPING WHITE AN ALL-WHITE ROOM GAINS DEPTH AND DIMENSION WITH A CREATIVE ARCHITECTURAL TREATMENT. A FALSE CORNICE HIDES THE DRAPERY TRACK ABOVE THE WINDOW WALL ON THE RIGHT, WHILE A DROPPED MOLDED PANEL CONCEALS THE CURTAIN MECHANICS OVER THE FRENCH DOORS ON THE LEFT. SANDWICHING THE DRAPERIES BETWEEN THE WALL AND THE INTERIOR MOLDING CREATES A LAYERED EFFECT THAT SOFTENS THE ARCHITECTURE WHILE PRESERVING THE SERENE ENVELOPE OF WHITE.

FLOOR-TO-CEILING SENSATION ORDINARY TIE-TAB SHEERS GAIN IMPORTANCE WHEN HUNG FROM IRON DRAPERY HOOKS INSTALLED IN THE CEILING. PUDDLING ON THE FLOOR, THE SHEERS EMPHASIZE THE HEIGHT IN THIS TROPICS-INSPIRED BEDROOM AND DOWNPLAY THE INEXPENSIVE PLEATED SHADE THAT PROVIDES PRIVACY.

VALANCES & SWAGS
Playful...Polished

TALKING POINTS TAKE IT FROM THE TOP—VALANCES AND SWAGS ARE FLOUNCY, FRIVOLOUS, AND UTTERLY APPEALING. MOST OFTEN THEY LEND A FINISHING TOUCH TO A WINDOW TREATMENT, BUT THEY ALSO CAN STAND ALONE, CROWNING THE WINDOW. A HARLEQUIN VALANCE OVERLAYS THE UPPER WINDOWS WITH SHAPE AND A TOUCH OF COLOR, ALLOWING THE TALL CASEMENTS TO OPERATE WITHOUT OBSTRUCTION. THE VALANCE FEATURES TWO LAYERS OF TRIANGLES: SMALL, NEUTRAL-COLOR ONES IN THE BACK, WHICH ARE OVERLAPPED BY LARGE TRIANGLES BORDERED WITH CONTRASTING FABRIC AND TRIMMED WITH TASSELS.

TAILORED FORMAL WEAR IN THIS IVORY AND BLACK ROOM, IVORY LINEN SWAGS THE WINDOWS AND FALLS IN JABOT-STYLE FOLDS ALONG THE SIDES. A WIDE BLACK BORDER EDGED WITH A GOLD GREEK-KEY PATTERN OUTLINES THE SHAPE. BECAUSE THE SWAGS ARE PURELY DECORATIVE, BAMBOO BLINDS PROVIDE PRIVACY AND FILTER LIGHT.

DECORATIVE DISGUISE THE DETAILED MOLDING OF THE WINDOW FRAME IN THIS VICTORIAN-STYLE LIVING ROOM IS TOO PRETTY TO COVER. BY MOUNTING A CLASSIC TASSEL-TRIMMED SILK SWAG AND JABOT JUST BELOW THE FRAME, THE MOLDING APPEARS TO BECOME PART OF THE WINDOW TREATMENT. THE CURVED DRAPE OF THE SWAG IS A NOD TO THE SAME DESIGN ELEMENT FOUND ELSEWHERE IN THE ROOM: IN THE WALLPAPER BORDER, ALONG THE TOP OF THE BOOKCASE, AND AT THE TOP OF THE ARMOIRE.

EXTRA AND SPECIAL TRANSOMS RARELY REQUIRE TREATMENTS, BUT THESE STRAIGHT VALANCES IN LACY CORAL DO TURN UP THE DECORATING VOLUME IN A FRESH, CONVIVIAL LIVING ROOM. WITH SIMPLE PLEATS ON EACH SIDE AND CUSTOM-FITTED TO MOUNT INSIDE THE TRANSOM FRAMES, THE VALANCES ADD COLOR AND FORM WITHOUT BLOCKING THE LIGHT.

FLOWER POWER A FLOUNCY FLORAL SWAG OVER A STRAIGHT VALANCE STITCHED FROM SALMON AND WHITE GINGHAM FABRIC IS JUST ENOUGH EMBELLISHMENT FOR THE BAY WINDOW IN THIS PLEASANT BREAKFAST ROOM. GINGHAM ROSETTES, EACH ACCENTED WITH A FABRIC-COVERED BUTTON, CATCH THE SWAG INTO GENEROUS GATHERS, CREATING A ROW OF BLOSSOMS ACROSS THE BAY. THE KITCHEN WINDOW FEATURES THE SAME WINDOW TREATMENT, A SMALL TOUCH THAT TIES THE ROOMS TOGETHER.

Pelmets & Cornice Boxes
Tailored...Structural

THEATRICAL TOUCH FANTASY, WHIMSY, AND CHARM COME TO LIFE IN A ROOM THAT RECALLS 1930S GLAMOUR. ONE OF THE MOST EFFECTIVE ELEMENTS IN THIS DESIGN IS THE USE OF REFLECTIVE ACCESSORIES. THE CRYSTAL CHANDELIER, THE ANTIQUE MIRROR, AND THE ETCHED MIRRORED CORNICES CATCH LIGHT AND REFLECT IT, GIVING THE ROOM A LUMINOUS FEELING. FULL-LENGTH CURTAIN PANELS ARE LEFT SIMPLE SO AS NOT TO DETRACT FROM THEIR ORNATE TOPPERS.

...Pelmets & Cornice Boxes

OLD ENGLISH INFLUENCE
Curvy, fabric-covered lambrequins patterned after window treatments found in Old-English country houses rejuvenate ordinary double-hung windows. In addition to softening the windows' angular lines, the lambrequins draw the eye upward, adding visual height to a room that has an uncharacteristically low ceiling.

Pelmets & Cornice Boxes...

PLEATED PERFECTION WHICH CAME FIRST: THE PELMET OR THE CORNICE? THESE TERMS ARE OFTEN USED INTERCHANGEABLY TO DESCRIBE A FIXED, VALANCELIKE TOPPER THAT FRAMES A WINDOW TREATMENT AND DISGUISES ITS MECHANICS. TECHNICALLY, PELMETS ARE SHAPED FROM WOOD OR STIFF FABRIC CALLED BUCKRAM. THEY ARE COVERED IN FABRIC AND MOUNTED INSIDE OR OUTSIDE THE WINDOW FRAME. IN THIS ROOM WHERE ARTWORK IS THE MAIN ATTRACTION, SIMPLE PLEATED PELMETS CONSTRUCTED FROM LUXURIOUS RAW SILK ARE SPARE BUT STYLISH. PINCH-PLEAT DRAPERIES IN THE SAME WARM CAMEL COLOR SOLIDIFY THE LOOK—COMPLEMENTING RATHER THAN COMPETING WITH THE GALLERY-INSPIRED ATMOSPHERE.

RICH REFLECTION A MIRRORED CORNICE BECOMES MORE THAN A TOPPER FOR PLEATED CURTAIN PANELS—IT BECOMES AN ARCHITECTURAL FEATURE THAT VISUALLY EXPANDS THE WINDOW'S WIDTH WHILE ADDING A 1930S-STYLE GLAMOUR TO THE DECOR.

Shades, Blinds & Shutters
Versatile...Functional

BOTANICAL BLISS Streamlined and structured, bamboo blinds, combined with floor-to-ceiling panels of caramel and cream plaid taffeta, unify a wall of windows that are different sizes. Blinds are often paired with other types of window treatments because they can be unrolled for privacy or filtering light. Otherwise they roll up and out of sight. Made of natural bamboo, these blinds were an obvious choice to complement the palm-print fabric on the valances and sofa.

Shades, Blinds & Shutters...

ELEGANT UNDERSTUDY IN THIS TRADITIONAL LIVING ROOM, WOOD-SLAT BLINDS AND PINCH-PLEAT DRAPERIES BLEND WITH THE WALLS TO MAKE A QUIET BACKGROUND FOR FURNISHINGS. CONTRASTING HEADERS AND LEADING EDGES ON THE DRAPERIES PICK UP THE COLOR OF THE SOFA TO LEAD THE EYE FROM FLOOR TO CEILING, ENLARGING THE SPACE.

TRENDSETTING TRANSLUCENCE FITTED SHUTTERS OFFER AN UNUSUAL ALTERNATIVE TO CONVENTIONAL WINDOW TREATMENTS. SCREWED DIRECTLY TO THE FRAMES OF CASEMENT-STYLE WINDOWS, THESE IRON FRAMES ARE SCREENED WITH TRANSLUCENT FIBERGLAS PAPER, THE SAME MATERIAL INCORPORATED INTO MODERN SHOJI SCREENS.

RESTRAINED FORMALITY MIDNIGHT BLUE WALLS CREATE THE DRAMA IN THIS DIN-
ING ROOM, WHILE WHITE SLAT BLINDS ADD REFINEMENT TO THE MIX. ALTHOUGH SOME STYLES
CAN BE PURCHASED READY-MADE, THESE BLINDS ARE CUSTOM-FITTED TO THE WINDOW—A
SOMETIMES EXPENSIVE BUT ATTRACTIVE BENEFIT IF YOU HAVE ODD-SHAPE WINDOWS. THE
DECORATIVE TAPES ARE ALSO CUSTOM, WITH A GREEK-KEY MOTIF THAT ADDS A DISTINCTIVE
PERSONAL TOUCH.

SHIPSHAPE CURVED LIKE THE BOW OF A SHIP, THE BOW WINDOW (A BAY WITH MORE THAN THREE SECTIONS) HINTS AT THIS LIBRARY'S OCEANSIDE LOCATION. TAILORED ROMAN SHADES FITTED INSIDE THE FRAMES OF THE NARROW WINDOWS DRAW UP IN FLAT FOLDS FOR A SLEEK, TAILORED LOOK, A GOOD SOLUTION FOR CASUAL LIVING SPACES.

WINDOW JEWELRY
Fashionable...Creative

HOOKED ON STYLE Simple linen valances are the perfect toppers for a series of French doors. Because a decorative rod might weigh down the look, the valances are suspended from modest hooks screwed into the top of the wall. Their placement also makes it easy to open and close the doors without the treatments getting in the way.

ACCENTUATE THE POSITIVE ARCHED WINDOWS ARE DISTINCTIVE ARCHITEC-
TURAL FEATURES, AND WINDOW TREATMENTS NEED TO BE CAREFULLY DESIGNED TO MAXIMIZE
THEIR IMPACT. THIS ANTIQUE IRON ROD WAS ORIGINAL TO THE HOUSE (SEE PAGE 76), BUT AN
IRONMONGER COULD CUSTOM-DESIGN SOMETHING SIMILAR FOR A NEW HOME. IRON RINGS
ALLOW LIGHTWEIGHT COTTON PANELS TO HANG IN LOOSE FOLDS FOR A FRESH, MODERN LOOK.

KEY TO SUCCESS CURTAIN PANELS HUNG WELL ABOVE THE WINDOW NEED A STRONG DESIGN ELEMENT TO MAKE THE LOOK EFFECTIVE. HERE CUSTOM IRON FINIALS IN A CLASSIC GREEK KEY SHAPE DO THE TRICK, DRAWING THE EYE UPWARD AND ADDING STRENGTH AND HEIGHT TO THE TREATMENT.

PRETTY IN A PINCH

GETTING THE LATEST LOOK HAS NEVER BEEN EASIER THANKS TO INNOVATIVE PRODUCTS IN TODAY'S MARKET. IN THIS CASE PURCHASED CURTAIN PANELS ARE ACCESSORIZED WITH IRON CURTAIN RINGS THAT SIMPLY CLIP TO THE TOP OF THE CURTAIN.

HANDSOME HEFT A BOLD AND BRASH BEDROOM PULLS IDEAS FROM THE PAST TO MAKE A SUCCESS OF ECLECTIC FURNISHINGS AND FABRICS. CHUNKY CURTAIN RINGS ARE A THROWBACK TO THE NATURAL, EARTHY DECORATING STYLE OF THE 1970S AND BALANCE THE STRONG VERTICAL IMPACT OF STRIPED, PINCH-PLEAT DRAPERIES. THE RODS ARE EXTRA LONG SO THE CURTAINS CAN BE PULLED COMPLETELY TO THE SIDES. THIS ALLOWS THE PLANTATION SHUTTERS TO BE FULLY OPERABLE.

FLORAL FINISH Overscale gilded wooden rods and curtain rings create solid frames for the top of these window treatments, but it is the ornate floral finials that capture the eye.

FRENCH TWIST WHEN IT COMES TO FRENCH DECOR, MORE EMBELLISHMENT DEFINITELY IS BETTER, AS ILLUSTRATED WITH THESE FABULOUSLY FLOUNCY CURTAINS. A CONTRAST TO THE STREAMLINED PLANTATION SHUTTERS, A GATHERED AND POUFED VALANCE EDGED WITH HEAVY WOODEN TASSELS DRESSES UP THE TREATMENT, WHILE EXTRA-LONG DAMASK PANELS ARE INTENTIONALLY UNLINED TO HANG LOOSELY AND PUDDLE TO THE FLOOR. THE CROWNING TOUCH? A ROW OF ORNATE FLOWER-SHAPE HOOKS TO HOLD THE VALANCE IN PLACE.

HANDSOME HOLDBACKS AN ELEGANT HOLDBACK MAKES ALL THE DIFFERENCE TO THIS WINDOW TREATMENT. THE DRAPERY IS SIMPLICITY ITSELF, A SINGLE LINED PANEL SLIPPED ONTO A SLENDER CURTAIN ROD. THE LOOK OF LUXURY COMES FROM THE ABUNDANCE OF FABRIC—AT LEAST TWO TIMES THE WINDOW WIDTH SHIRRED SNUGLY ONTO THE ROD. THE HOLDBACK GATHERS THE FABRIC INTO WEIGHTY FOLDS, AND IF PRIVACY IS DESIRED, THE DRAPERY CAN BE ALLOWED TO FALL STRAIGHT FROM THE ROD.

TIEBACKS & HOLDBACKS
Practical...Decorative

DAINTY DETAIL AN EMBOSSED AND ETCHED ANTIQUE HOLDBACK KEEPS PALE PINK PINSTRIPED CURTAINS GATHERED IN SOFT FOLDS AT THE SIDE OF A WINDOW. HOLDBACKS SHOULD BE MOUNTED ON THE WINDOW FRAME SO THE POINT OF ATTACHMENT IS HIDDEN BY THE DRAPERIES, WHETHER THEY ARE PULLED BACK OR ALLOWED TO CLOSE.

THE POWER of STYLE / TAPERT and EDKINS

SCULPTURE
FROM ANTIQUITY TO THE PRESENT DAY

CAROLYNE ROEHM *Summer* NOTEBOOK

PEOPLE PEARLS

20,000 YEARS OF FASHION

TAILORED ALTERNATIVE

THE FIXED FOLDS ON THESE ELE-
GANT CURTAINS REQUIRE NEITHER
A TIEBACK NOR A HOLDBACK, YET
THEY SERVE THE SAME FUNCTION—
TO DRAW ASIDE THE PANELS FROM
THE WINDOW. CALLED "ITALIAN
STRINGING," THE TECHNIQUE IS
EXECUTED BY STRINGING NYLON
CORD THROUGH PLASTIC RINGS
STITCHED TO THE BACK OF THE
PANELS TO CREATE THE FOLDS.

TASSELED TIEBACKS A CARAMEL-COLOR DRAPERY IN A RICH SILK FABRIC NEEDS NO EMBELLISHMENT FOR A LUXURIOUS LOOK. INSTEAD, THE SINGLE DRAPERY IS PULLED TO ONE SIDE AND CASUALLY CAUGHT UP IN HEAVY TASSELS IN THE SAME RICH HUE.

7 WALL COVERINGS

Nothing is as daunting or as exciting to an artist as the possibilities presented by a blank canvas. Plain walls evoke the same feeling. Choosing the subject for a wall-size mural or decorative wallpaper—not to mention a single paint color—can be fraught with angst, but indecisiveness and worry fade when the decision is made and the result turns out to be spectacular!

To choose which treatment to try, study wall finishes, visit designer showhouses, and spend time in paint stores familiarizing yourself with the new wallpapers, textures, techniques, and treatments. With patience and a willingness to experiment and explore through trial and error, you will find the perfect treatment.

HAND-PAINTED PERFECTION

TRADITIONAL HARDLY MEANS TRITE, AS EVIDENCED IN THIS STATELY DINING ROOM. TO BALANCE FORMALITY, A HAND-PAINTED WALLPAPER IN DEEP YELLOW BRINGS A LIGHT FEEL AND SENSE OF REFINEMENT TO THE ROOM. THE SOFT BLUES, GREENS, GRAYS, AND PINKS ARE DOMINANT IN THE SILK TAFFETA DRAPERIES, BUT THE WALL-PAPER EXPRESSES THE COLOR PALETTE IN AN ENTIRELY DIFFERENT PRESENTATION.

DECORATIVE FINSHES
Evocative...
Illusory...Imaginative

AGING GRACEFULLY A TWIST ON THE TRADITIONAL FAUX FINISH OF AGED PLASTER IS APPLIED TO THE WALLS OF THIS COLORFUL DINING ROOM. INSTEAD OF STICKING TO ONE COLOR FOR THE FINISH, LAYERS OF GOLD, SAGE GREEN, AND TANGERINE ARE RANDOMLY RUBBED ONTO THE WALLS IN A MANNER THAT LETS EACH COLOR PEEK THROUGH. THE GOAL IS TO SUGGEST THAT LAYERS OF COLOR HAVE BEEN APPLIED OVER TIME AND THEN HAVE BEEN WORN AWAY.

Decorative Finishes...

CREATIVE COMBINATION A COMBINATION OF DECORATIVE FINISHES IMPARTS GRANDEUR TO THIS SMALL DINING ROOM. ABOVE THE CHAIR RAIL, WALLS ARE GLAZED WITH A SUNNY PUMPKIN PATINA. BELOW THE CHAIR RAIL, OLIVE AND ANTIQUE YELLOW ARE SPONGED FOR A SOFTLY MOTTLED EFFECT. ON THE FLOOR, YELLOW AND GREEN PAINT SIMULATE THE LOOK OF A PATTERNED CARPET. THE FIREPLACE GAINS NEW IMPORTANCE WITH A FAUX MARBLE FINISH ON THE HEARTH AND FIREBOX SURROUND.

FAUX GRASS CLOTH A KITCHEN GAINS INSTANT PERSONALITY WHEN THE WALLS ARE COMBED TO RESEMBLE GRASS CLOTH, A WALLCOVERING THAT WAS POPULAR IN THE 1950S. THE TREATMENT PROVIDES A VIVID BACKDROP FOR THE KITCHEN'S DRAPERIES AND GRANITE COUNTERTOPS. TO ACHIEVE THE LOOK, RED-TINTED GLAZE IS BRUSHED OVER A BEIGE EGGSHELL-FINISH LATEX BASE COAT AND COMBED VERTICALLY WITH A NOTCHED SQUEEGEE. AFTER THE FIRST COAT DRIES, A SECOND COAT OF GLAZE IS APPLIED AND COMBED HORIZONTALLY.

VENERABLE VENETIAN PLASTER Timeworn textures and earthy hues imbue this hallway with the character of a centuries-old stone cottage perched on a Tuscan hillside. The faded patina is the result of a clay-color Venetian plaster technique. Walls are layered with an interior stucco and plaster compound that is tinted with dry raw umber and troweled on in thin coats. Hand-painted scrolled images and rubbed beeswax add flourish to the finish.

Decorative Finishes...

STIPPLED SERENITY A BLUE LIVING ROOM INTERPRETS MODERN DESIGN THROUGH SOPHISTICATED, SERENE COLORS THAT SOOTHE RATHER THAN SHOCK. WALLS ARE PAINTED AN IDYLLIC GRAY-BLUE AND LIGHTLY STIPPLED IN A HUE ONE SHADE DARKER FOR DEPTH. A LIGHTER BLUE ON THE CEILING DRAWS ATTENTION UPWARD TO ENLARGE THE SENSE OF SPACE.

SPONGED FOR SUBTLETY GLAZED HERON-BLUE WALLS ARE SPONGED AND RUBBED WITH WHITE-TINTED GLAZE FOR A CLOUDLIKE EFFECT. LAYERING GLAZES OF TWO SIMILAR TONES GIVES THE WALLS A PLEASING DEPTH YET ALLOWS ATTENTION TO FOCUS ON THE ARTWORK RATHER THAN THE WALL TREATMENT. A HAND-PAINTED GARDEN TRELLIS DESIGN ON THE FLOOR ELIMINATES THE NEED FOR A RUG.

...Decorative Finishes

GLAZED FOR GLAMOUR A DECORATIVE PAINT FINISH NEED NOT BE APPLIED TO ALL OF THE WALLS. INSTEAD, IT CAN HIGHLIGHT A FOCAL POINT, SUCH AS THIS BEDROOM'S FIREPLACE WALL. FOR A SHIMMERING METALLIC FINISH, A WARM COPPER GLAZE WAS BRUSHED OVER A METALLIC BASE COAT IN A SERIES OF SWEEPING, OVERLAPPING ARCS. THE RESULT ADDS DEPTH AND MOVEMENT TO THE LAYERS OF TEXTURES IN THE ROOM.

Decorative Finishes...

STUCCOED WITH STYLE

Crumbly stucco-style walls infuse this eating area with the cozy allure of an old farmhouse kitchen. Shades of terra-cotta glaze applied with crumpled plastic wrap let the sunny yellow base coat peek through—a technique that produces an aged effect but keeps the room from becoming too dark.

WALLPAPER Enveloping...Patterned... Intricate...Eye-Catching

WONDERS WITH WALLPAPER

COMBINING SEVERAL TYPES OF WALLPA-
PER CREATES A PROMENADE OF PATTERN
THAT MAKES THIS BEDROOM ELEGANT AND
INTERESTING. MARBLED PAPER IN A RICH
GOLDEN HUE COVERS THE CEILING, WHILE
THE WALLS FEATURE A SUBTLE YELLOW
STRIPE TOPPED WITH A 12-INCH CLASSIC
BORDER. TO CALL ATTENTION TO THE WIN-
DOWS, CORNICES ARE PAINTED WITH A
BLACK-AND-GOLD MOTIF, GLAZED TO COM-
PLEMENT THE WALLS, AND CROWNED WITH
A DEFINING BAND OF BLACK MOLDING.

Wallpaper...

PLAY ON PATTERN WALLPAPER PACKS A PUNCH FOR ITS ABILITY TO ADD TEXTURE, COLOR, AND DETAIL TO AN INTERIOR. IT IS ALSO VERSATILE—USING THE SAME PAPER IN DIFFERENT SETTINGS AND ARRANGEMENTS OFTEN CAN PRODUCE DRAMATICALLY DIFFERENT RESULTS. FOR THIS SMALL BEDROOM, THE FOREST GREEN DAMASK-PATTERN WALLPAPER IS ROMANTIC AND SERENE, A FITTING BACKDROP FOR AN EDWARDIAN-STYLE INTERIOR.

VIVACIOUS WALLS IF YOU LOVE PATTERN, WRAP YOUR ROOM IN IT. THIS EXTRAVAGANT HOMAGE TO BLUE AND WHITE PORCELAIN CREATES THE ILLUSION OF DEPTH BECAUSE THE IMAGES FLOAT AGAINST A TAN BACKGROUND. REAL BLUE AND WHITE PORCELAIN SEEMS TO EMERGE FROM THE PATTERN, ENHANCING THE EFFECT.

207

DECORATIVE DECEPTION

WALLPAPER HAS AN ILLUSIONAL ASPECT THAT ALLOWS IT TO LOOK ONE WAY FROM ONE PERSPECTIVE AND COMPLETELY DIFFERENT FROM ANOTHER. IN THIS CHEERFUL SITTING AREA, THE WALLS ARE PAPERED WITH WHAT SEEMS TO BE GRASS CLOTH. UPON CLOSER INSPECTION, HOWEVER, THE WALLPAPER IS ACTUALLY A PRINT OF FINE ROPE THAT STRETCHES FROM FLOOR TO CEILING. ANOTHER TRICK EMPLOYED HERE IS ADDING A DECORATIVE WALLPAPER BORDER AROUND THE CEILING, AN EFFECT THAT HEIGHTENS WALLS.

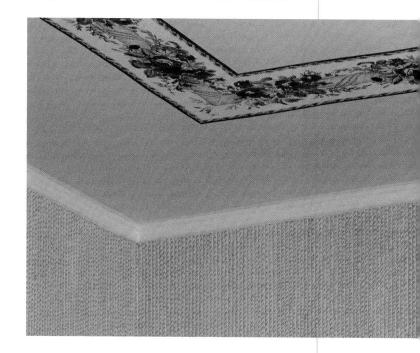

STENCILS & HAND-PAINTING

REFINEMENT IN RELIEF

EMBOSSED PLASTER WALLS BRING DEPTH AND TEXTURE TO THIS DINING ROOM. THE HIGH RELIEF IS ACHIEVED BY USING GENEROUS AMOUNTS OF PLASTER. THE FIRST COAT WAS APPLIED ALL OVER. AFTER IT DRIED, MORE PLASTER WAS TROWELED THROUGH A STENCIL TO CREATE THE LOW-RELIEF EFFECT. TWO COATS OF GOLDEN GLAZE WERE THEN BRUSHED ON TO ACCENTUATE THE PATTERN AND HIGHLIGHT THE RICH TEXTURE OF THE ROYAL PURPLE DRAPERIES.

SWEET REPEATS REMINISCENT OF SKY, SEA, EARTH, AND RAIN, THE WELCOMING PALETTE OF THIS COASTAL COTTAGE ENTRY REFLECTS THE COLORS OF THE SEASIDE. TOO BRIGHT AND THE EFFECT WOULD BE GAUDY AND OVERDONE; TOO WHITE AND THE ROOM WOULD BE STARK AND UNINVITING. JUST RIGHT IS A ROOM OF CREAMY WHITE TINTED WITH SEA-MIST GREEN. STENCILED BANDS OF DAMASK MOTIFS ALONG WITH SMALLER AVIAN FORMS CREATE A DECORATIVE COMPOSITION THAT IS BOTH SHABBY AND CHIC.

Stencils & Hand-Painting...

PAINTED WITH PERSONALITY

HAND-PAINTING LENDS AN INDIVIDUALITY TO MURALS THAT CANNOT BE MATCHED BY PURCHASED WALLPAPER. INSPIRED BY PASTORAL NEW ENGLAND, THE WALL-SIZE MURAL IN THIS FORMAL DINING ROOM IS DEFINITELY A CONVERSATION STARTER, ESPECIALLY WHEN GUESTS REALIZE THAT REFERENCES TO THE OWNERS' FAVORITE PLACES AND PETS ARE IMMORTALIZED IN IT. THE MURAL IS DONE IN ACRYLIC PAINTS AND FINISHED WITH A CLEAR PROTECTIVE VARNISH TO GUARD AGAINST SOILING AND FADING.

SERENE SCENE CONTRARY TO WHAT YOU MIGHT EXPECT, SMALL ROOMS ARE IDEAL FOR LARGE DECORATIVE EFFECTS. HERE A HAND-PAINTED MURAL ENVELOPS A SMALL POWDER ROOM WITH HIGH DRAMA. EXECUTED IN THE HUDSON RIVER SCHOOL-STYLE, THE MURAL IS GLAZED AND CRACKLED TO PRODUCE AN AGED FINISH.

FASHIONABLE FRAME A HAND-PAINTED FRAME EMBELLISHED WITH WINDING VINES AND FLITTING BUTTERFLIES ADDS COUNTRY CHARM TO A SCANDINAVIAN-STYLE BEDROOM. RATHER THAN COVER THE ENTIRE WALL, THE FRAME IS POSITIONED TO ACCENT THE BED AND SUGGEST ARCHITECTURAL DETAIL WHERE NONE EXISTS.

FREEHAND FLORALS THE SOARING CEILING IN THIS CHILD'S BEDROOM IS VISUALLY LOWERED BY THE HAND-PAINTED FLORAL MOTIF FLOATING ON A CREAMY BACKGROUND ABOVE THE WOOD TRIM. THE RASPBERRY FLOWERS ARE PAINTED RANDOMLY BY HAND TO MATCH THE BEDSPREAD, WITH GREEN VINES AND LEAVES ADDED FOR CONTRAST.

TRIMS & MOLDING Architectual...Rich... Defining...Elegant

DEFINITIVE PANELS ONCE PASSÉ, PANELED WALLS HAVE BEEN REVIVED BY HOMEOWNERS WHO ADMIRE THEIR DIMENSIONAL ASPECTS. PAINTED A DISTINCTIVE HUE SIMILAR TO THAT OF RED-ORANGE POPPIES, THE PANELS IN THIS COUNTRY-CHIC LIVING ROOM ADD CHARACTER TO THE WALLS. A WIDE SHELF ABOVE THE DOOR FORMS A VISUAL SEPARATION, CALLING ATTENTION TO THE ROOM'S ARCHED CEILING.

FRAMED FOR DEFINITION IN AN OCTAGONAL DINING ROOM FEATURING CHAIRS WITH FRUIT-MOTIF FABRIC UPHOLSTERY, A SERIES OF HAND-PAINTED PANELS OF CITRUS ENTWINED WITH LEAVES AND BRANCHES RINGS THE TOP OF THE CEILING. MOLDING FRAMES THE PAINTINGS, GIVING THEM THE LOOK OF BOTANICAL PRINTS.

PICTURE RAIL A CUSTOM-DESIGNED BANQUETTE GETS A SHOT OF PERSONAL STYLE WITH PICTURE-FRAME MOLDINGS THAT STAY TRUE TO THEIR NAME. MOUNTED JUST ABOVE WINDOW HEIGHT, THE MOLDINGS ARE SEPARATED BY 4 INCHES, THE STANDARD SIZE FOR SNAPSHOTS. PHOTOS CAN BE POPPED IN AND OUT OF THE BORDER AS DESIRED.

DOUBLE REFLECTION MIRRORS INJECT GLAMOUR AND DEPTH INTO AN INTERIOR. IN THIS NARROW LIVING ROOM, PANELS OF MIRRORS ARE MOUNTED BEHIND THE SOFA TO INCREASE THE SENSE OF HEIGHT AND DEPTH. AN OCTAGONAL MIRROR WITH A GILT FRAME FLOATS IN THE CENTER OF THE PANELS, ADDING ANOTHER LAYER OF ILLUSION AND DEPTH.

Mirrors...

FRENCH APPEAL Louis XVI-style wall panels, architectural moldings, and mirrored doors and walls transform a living room into a Parisian pied-à-terre. The walls and ceiling are lacquered in high gloss to bounce shimmery natural light in all directions. Mirrored panels on the wall behind the sofa amplify the effect and add visual depth to the room.

OPTICAL EFFECTS THE MULTIPLICATION OF REFLECTIONS MAKES IT HARD TO TELL WHERE ONE WALL JOINS ANOTHER IN THIS BATHROOM, ELOQUENT TESTIMONY TO THE POWER OF MIRRORS TO EXPAND A SMALL SPACE. HANGING A FRAMED MIRROR OVER THE MIRRORED SINK WALL BREAKS UP THE REFLECTION WITH WARM WOOD THAT LINKS CABINETS TO CEILING.

WITTY WALL ART This functional and fun backsplash combines standard 4-inch-square tiles for the wall with a border of black and white 2-inch squares at the base. Decorative plates embedded in the adhesive along with the tile give the wall a European look. Wider-than-usual grout lines emphasize its rustic character.

VERSATILITY OF TILE
Streamlined...Classic...Clean...Spare

TAILORED EFFECT DIAMOND-SHAPE TILES CUT FROM NATURAL STONE AND SET SNUGLY (WITH NO GROUT LINES SHOWING) FORM AN ELEGANT BACKSPLASH IN THIS EUROPEAN-STYLE KITCHEN. TILES ARE A POPULAR CHOICE FOR KITCHENS BECAUSE THEY ARE DURABLE AND EASY TO CLEAN.

FACETS OF FABRIC Unexpected... Understated...Textured

ENVELOPED IN FABRIC MAKING A DRAMATIC STATEMENT IN TRADITIONAL STYLE IS THE IMPETUS FOR UPHOLSTERING WALLS IN THIS LARGE AND LIGHT BEDROOM. THE PANELS STRETCH FROM FLOOR TO CEILING MOLDINGS AND ARE A DEEP CREAMY SILK TO GIVE THE WALLS A SHEEN. THE LIGHTLY TUFTED HARLEQUIN PATTERN IS CREATED BY STRIPS OF CONTRASTING RIBBED-COTTON RIBBONS ATTACHED WITH HARD-EDGE NAILHEADS.

CURTAIN CALL SIMPLE GATHERED CURTAIN PANELS STITCHED FROM WASHABLE FABRIC WRAP AROUND THIS SMALL COTTAGE BATH TO HIDE LESS-THAN-PERFECT WALLS. THE RESULT HAS A ROMANTIC AND LUXURIOUS EFFECT ON SUCH A CONFINED SPACE.

LUXURIOUS LINEN THE ENTIRE WALL BECOMES AN UPHOLSTERED HEADBOARD IN THIS CONTEMPORARY BEDROOM. PANELS OF TAUPE LINEN STRETCHED OVER PADDING ARE MOUNTED TO THE WALL. MATCHING PAINT COVERS THE REMAINING WALLS TO CREATE A QUIET COCOON OF NEUTRAL COLOR.

PRETTY BUT PRACTICAL

There are times when function and necessity trump beauty. Consider a wall with major flaws in the plaster. Or perhaps a window is original to the house and therefore lacks energy-efficient panes. Some obstacles have no permanent remedy, such as homes lacking a decent view or south-facing windows where sunlight seems never-ending.

When immediate repairs are not an option, the next best thing is to explore innovative ways to disguise the problem or draw attention away from it. Luckily, the solution also can be smart and sophisticated, as shown in the pretty but practical rooms featured in this chapter.

EYE-CATCHING FLOURISH IN A ROOM WITH UNEXCEPTIONAL ARCHITECTURE AND A WALL OF BIG WINDOWS, AN ARCHED WINDOW TREATMENT—PART CORNICE, PART VALANCE—STEALS THE SHOW. THE FRAME IS CURVED WOOD MOUNTED ABOVE THE WINDOW FOR HEIGHT. THE SILK VALANCE IS FITTED AND PLEATED DIRECTLY ONTO THE CORNICE, WITH CORDING TO FINISH THE EDGES AND FULL-LENGTH DRAPERIES TO FRAME THE VIEW.

POINT OF VIEW THE VIEW IS LESS THAN DESIRABLE, BUT COVERING THE WINDOW ELIM-
INATES NATURAL LIGHT IN THE ROOM. WHAT TO DO? ONE SOLUTION IS TO HANG A CONTINUOUS
FULL-LENGTH PANEL OVER THE WINDOWS AND FOLD BACK ONE CORNER TO THE MIDDLE SEC-
TION OF THE CURTAIN. THE RESULT CREATES AN INTERESTING ALLURE, HIDES A MAJORITY OF
THE VIEW, AND LETS LIGHT PEEK THROUGH THE EXPOSED PORTION OF THE WINDOW.

SENSE OF PRIVACY DINING BEHIND SHEER CURTAINS TIED BACK WITH TASSELS TRANSFORMS EVERY MEAL INTO A ROMANTIC AFFAIR. THE CURTAINS' PRIMARY PURPOSE IS TO PROVIDE PRIVACY BY SEPARATING THE DINING ROOM, WHICH HAS NO DOORS, FROM THE REST OF THE KITCHEN. YET THE LOOK ALSO DEFINES THE ENTRANCE TO THE ROOM AND BECOMES A FOCAL POINT IN THE DECOR.

Pretty but Practical...

DAINTY VEIL IN A SMALL BEDROOM, PURCHASED SHEERS HANG FROM SWING-ARM RODS TO SUGGEST AN EXTENSION OF THE WALL. ONE ALSO DOUBLES AS A WINDOW TREATMENT. THE RODS CAN SWING CLOSED TO HIDE THE CLOSET DOOR, A PRACTICAL MEASURE IF THE DOOR IS ILL-FITTING OR IF YOU WANT TO SOFTEN THE ARCHITECTURE.

AWKWARD TO AWESOME A DORMER IN AN UPSTAIRS GUEST ROOM BECOMES AN ALTERNATIVE SPOT FOR BREAKFAST OR LUNCH WITH A SMALL TABLE AND A PAIR OF CHAIRS. TO FILTER LIGHT, A DOUBLE-SIDED, FULL-LENGTH PANEL OF BLACK SILK ORGANZA IS MOUNTED INSIDE THE WINDOW FRAME. BRONZE SILK VALANCES ARE POSITIONED 12 AND 24 INCHES IN FRONT OF THE PANEL, CREATING A LAYERED EFFECT. THE STEPPING-OUT TECHNIQUE MAKES THE 5-FOOT DORMER APPEAR SHALLOWER AND PROVIDES A SNAPPY CONTEMPORARY BACK-DROP FOR MODERN FURNISHINGS.

WROUGHT-IRON TRACERY A WROUGHT-IRON CHANDELIER IS THE STARTING POINT FOR A DECORATIVE THEME IN THIS DINING ROOM. A PIECE OF SALVAGED WROUGHT-IRON FENCING HANGS UPSIDE DOWN AS A FLOURISH OVER THE SMALL WINDOW, WHILE AN IRON ROD HOLDS SHEER CAFE CURTAINS AT THE LARGER SET OF WINDOWS. SECURED TO THE ROD WITH CURTAIN CLIPS, THE PANEL CAN BE EXCHANGED EASILY FOR A HEAVIER TREATMENT IN WINTER.

Pretty but Practical...

CLEVER COVER-UP TURN FLAWED WALLS INTO STUNNING WORKS OF ART. IN THIS TRA-
DITIONAL LIVING ROOM WITH CONTEMPORARY TOUCHES, A REPLICA OF A LEONARDO DA VINCI
BOTANICAL WAS TRANSFERRED TO A LARGE SHEET OF ARTIST'S PAPER, BURNED AND TORN
AROUND THE EDGES TO SIMULATE WEAR AND TEAR, AND THEN APPLIED TO THE WALLS WITH
WALLPAPER PASTE. THE WALL WAS THEN COATED WITH A CRACKLE FINISH.

PRIVACY PLEASE   IN THIS CORRIDOR-STYLE BATHROOM, HEAVY CANVAS SHOWER CURTAINS DOUBLE AS A ROOM DIVIDER TO CLOSE OFF THE BATH AREA FOR PRIVACY. THE VINTAGE TUB IS OUTFITTED WITH A HANDHELD SHOWERHEAD, SO ONE CURTAIN FITS INSIDE THE TUB TO PROTECT THE WALL OF STORAGE. THE PRIVACY CURTAIN HANGS TO THE FLOOR. THE CURTAIN RODS, SUSPENDED FROM THE CEILING, CAN BE ASSEMBLED FROM PIPES, JOINTS, AND FITTINGS FOUND AT ANY HOME IMPROVEMENT CENTER.

WARM AND WELCOMING

STRONG AND BOLD, RED-CHECKED ROMAN SHADES PULL UP TO SHOWCASE VIEWS OF THE GARDEN BUT CAN BE LOWERED TO THE FLOOR TO KEEP THIS CHEERFUL SUNROOM WARM DURING THE WINTER. THE SHADES ARE LINED WITH COTTON AND INTERLINED WITH A FELTLIKE MATERIAL THAT FORMS AN ADDITIONAL BARRIER AGAINST COLD AND HELPS THE SHADES HANG BETTER BY ADDING FULLNESS TO THE FOLDS.

Pretty but Practical...

DISTINCTIVE DIFFUSION NATURAL
LIGHT IS A GLORIOUS ASSET TO A ROOM, BUT
DURING THE HOTTEST AND BRIGHTEST TIMES
OF THE DAY, FILTERING HEAT AND LIGHT
BECOMES ESSENTIAL TO MAINTAIN COMFORT.
A WELL-APPOINTED SCREEN PORCH-TURNED-
FAMILY ROOM FEATURES WINDOWS CROWNED
WITH HANDSOME ALL-WHITE CANVAS COR-
NICES THAT BRING THE WHITE OF THE CEILING
DOWN THE WALL. FULL-LENGTH SHEERS CAN
BE PULLED ACROSS WINDOWS AS FILTERS OR
FASTENED TO THE SIDES WHEN NOT NEEDED.

...Pretty but Practical

FABRIC FOCUS LARGE, CAVERNOUS ROOMS ARE COMMON IN NEW HOMES, LEAVING HOMEOWNERS SEARCHING FOR WAYS TO MAKE SUCH OVERWHELMING SPACES MORE INVITING. IN THIS BEDROOM THE VISUAL SPACE SHRINKS WHEN FLOOR-LENGTH DRAPERIES AND DEEP CORNICES IN A LARGE FLORAL PRINT FRAME THE WINDOWS. THE BOLD COLOR DRAWS YOUR EYE SO YOU DON'T NOTICE THE TOO-LARGE DIMENSIONS OF THE ROOM. NEUTRAL FABRIC WOULD HAVE THE OPPOSITE EFFECT, MAKING THE WINDOWS SEEM FARTHER AWAY FROM THE BED.

CAPITALIZE ON TALL AND THIN AVOID OVERDRESSING SLIM BUT SOARING WINDOWS. TOO FUSSY A TREATMENT WOULD HIDE THE ELONGATED SHAPE; TOO SPARE AND THE LOOK CAN BE STARK AND COLD. ONE NO-FAIL WAY TO MAKE A STATEMENT IS TO PAIR FABRICS IN FABULOUS TEXTURES AND SOFT COLORS WITH SIMPLE PANELS AND HARDWARE, AN EFFECT THAT EMPHASIZES THIS WINDOW'S CLASSIC LINES.

CHIC SEPARATION USED TO DEFINE INTERIOR SPACE, RED SHEERS WITH BOLD BLACK BORDERS INJECT UNEXPECTED DRAMA INTO THIS HALLWAY. ALSO KNOWN AS A PORTIERE, THE HALL PANEL HANGS FROM SMALL RINGS ON A SLIM ROD INSTALLED IN THE DOORWAY. A MATCHING PANEL PARTIALLY COVERS THE WINDOW ON THE FAR WALL, CREATING A SYMMETRICAL EFFECT AND PULLING THE EYE THROUGH THE SPACE.

Pretty but Practical...

REFRESHED FORMALITY ALTHOUGH FURNISHINGS CAN DO WONDERS FOR AN OTHERWISE DULL INTERIOR, ARCHITECTURAL DETAILS ELEVATE A ROOM'S GRANDEUR AND SPLENDOR, AS ILLUSTRATED IN THIS ELEGANTLY APPOINTED ENGLISH-STYLE SITTING ROOM. THE PERIOD-STYLE CROWN MOLDING, WHICH ADDS POLISH AND PANACHE, IS FASHIONED FROM 5-INCH BASIC CROWN AND PICTURE-RAIL MOLDING. WOOD FLORETS RUBBED WITH GOLD PASTE ARE GLUED IN PLACE BETWEEN THE MOLDINGS.

SHUTTERED SOLUTION

Antique wood grates from Bali solve two problems in this kitchen's eat-in dining area: their intricately carved form becomes artwork in a room with no significant wall space for display, and they serve as shutters for a set of windows without blocking much needed light from the room.

...Pretty but Practical

EXPANDING THE STRAIGHT AND NARROW Spatial interest is almost nil in a long and narrow room. To combat the bowling-alley aura and create the illusion of more height, deep crown molding with a shimmering metallic finish draws the eye upward, as do the curved edge and full length of the pleated draperies. The color combination of red and yellow is used liberally to make this space warm and inviting.

Pretty but Practical...

CONVERSION TO COMFORT

THIS SMALL ROOM WITH A SLANTED CEILING
HAD A CRAMPED AND CHOPPY FEEL BEFORE
ITS MAKEOVER. NOW WALLPAPER WITH A
SMALL FLORAL PATTERN DISGUISES THE MUL-
TIPLE ANGLES, DRAWS THE EYE AWAY FROM
THE LOW CEILING HEIGHT ALONG ONE WALL,
AND CREATES A COHESIVENESS THROUGH-
OUT THE ROOM. A STRAIGHT VALANCE AND
PLEATED ROMAN SHADES IN COTTAGE-STYLE
FABRICS BECOME THE FOCAL POINT.

BEAUTIFUL
EMBELLISHMENTS

Special finishes personalize your windows. Purchase ready-made window treatments and accent them with beads and baubles—even jewelry can be used for a stunning focal point. Likewise, the options for walls are vast. Choose a color you like and experiment with faux finishes, glazes, wallpaper, borders, and stencils to produce an individualized look.

THE TROPICS IN TEXTURE ON THIS SUNPORCH, NATURAL SHADES OF GREEN, BROWN, AND WHEAT IN A VARIETY OF TEXTURES SET A RUGGEDLY SOPHISTICATED TONE. POURED-CONCRETE PILLARS PROVIDE NEUTRAL-COLOR WALL SPACE BETWEEN THE BANKS OF WINDOWS, WHICH ARE TRIMMED IN PINE GREEN. SIMPLE HANDKERCHIEF SLIPS OF LOOSELY WOVEN COTTON DRAPE FROM BUNDLED BAMBOO RODS TO SOFTEN THE CORNER WINDOWS.

FRENCH COUTURE GIVING AN EFFECT SIMILAR TO ITALIAN STRINGING, LARGE DECORATIVE CLIPS PIN BACK VOLUPTUOUS SILK PANELS. THE DEEPLY SCALLOPED SHEERS UNDERNEATH ARE TRIMMED IN PEARL PENDANTS DANGLING FROM STRANDS OF GOLD BEADS. THE SHEERS EXUDE EXTRAVAGANCE BUT ALSO HAVE A PURPOSE: TO HIDE AN UNINSPIRING VIEW AND INFUSE THE ROOM WITH VICTORIAN-STYLE SOFTNESS.

NEEDLEPOINT PERFECTION THE WINDOW WALL UNDER A CATHEDRAL CEILING PROVIDES AN OPPORTUNITY TO FRAME ORDINARY WINDOWS WITH AN EXTRAORDINARY TREATMENT. ANTIQUE NEEDLEPOINT, ONCE THE SEAT FOR A PIANO STOOL, BECOMES THE CROWN OF A SUMPTUOUS SWAG AND CURTAIN PANELS. THE PANELS ARE FASHIONED FROM CRANBERRY POLISHED COTTON AND LINED WITH A MATCHING CHECK. LARGE GREEN TASSELS SUPPLY A FINISHING FLOURISH.

...Embellishments

RENDITION ON TRADITION

PLAYFUL TROMPE L'OEIL SWAGS OUTLINE THE CEILING BELOW TRADITIONAL-STYLE CROWN MOLDING IN THIS DINING ROOM. THE TREATMENT UNDERSCORES THE FEDERAL STYLE OF THE FURNISHINGS. THE MUTED RED AND WHITE OF THE SWAGS ARE THE SAME LOW-KEY VALUE AS THE BLUE ON THE WALLS, SO THE FOOL-THE-EYE TREATMENT DOESN'T CLAMOR FOR ATTENTION BUT SURPRISES THE EYE WITH AN UNEXPECTED DESIGN ELEMENT.

Embellishments...

TIP-TOP DETAILS A PINCH-PLEAT VALANCE GOES FROM PLAIN TO POSH WITH THE ADDITION OF HEAVY CORDING AND MULTI-COLOR POM-POM TRIM. ROPE CORD RUNS FROM ONE SIDE TO THE OTHER, WITH SIMPLE KNOTS AT EACH PLEAT. THE BOTTOM EDGE OF THE VALANCE IS SHAPED TO BREAK UP THE SQUARENESS OF THE SPACE, WITH CINCH PLEATS SOFTLY GATHERING THE FABRIC TO EMPHASIZE EACH POINT. POM-POM TASSELS HANG FROM FLAT BRAID FOR MOVEMENT.

OVER AND ABOVE Unusual denim-striped canopies stretch over the beds in this small alcove bedroom, an idea inspired by traditional campaign tents. Attached to simple metal curtain rods, the canopy embellishments transform the room's weakest design element—the steeply sloped ceiling—into an asset.

COUNTRY CHARM To show off the floor-to-ceiling windows in this dining bay, the windows are left uncovered, crowned only with pleated valances. These are a rich mix of elements: A pale green botanical with tassel fringe layered over blue and white toile and caught up with double bows fastened with covered buttons. Windows outside the bay wear toile curtains accented with pale green ties and banded with the green botanical print and a blue check.

ASTOUNDING AWNINGS ONE SHOW-STOPPING ELEMENT CAN TAKE A ROOM FROM PLEASANT TO EXTRAORDINARY. THIS LITTLE GIRL'S BEDROOM IS LOVELY AND FEMININE WITH LAVENDER WALLS, WHITE MOLDINGS, AND GENEROUS GREEN CHECK SHEERS AT THE WINDOWS. ADD THE DECORATIVE COTTON AWNINGS, AND THE ROOM ACQUIRES A PLAYFUL MOOD THAT ENCOURAGES FANTASY AND IMAGINATION.

CELESTIAL SETTING ADD REAL DIMENSION TO PLAIN WALLS WITH RESIN STARS HOT-GLUED IN A LOOSE BUT REGULAR PATTERN. THE STARS ARE GILDED WITH SILVER LEAF TO COORDINATE WITH THE DINING ROOM'S FIBERGLASS LIGHT FIXTURE TO CREATE A UNIFIED LOOK.

10 CREATIVE COMBINATIONS

Combining two types of window treatments, such as shutters or blinds with draperies, is a common way to enjoy the benefits of both: shutters and blinds may block light more effectively while draperies soften the architecture and add color to the room. In this chapter, however, you'll see ideas for applications that go beyond the expected. A perennial favorite such as curtain panels takes on new drama when hung from an unexpected height. A patterned wallpaper paired with a different but equally compelling print for windows brings fresh zest to a decorating scheme. Even the way you combine furnishings, accessories, and fabrics can elevate the strength of the design in a room. Don't be afraid to try new twists on tradition. When you trust your instincts, your ideas will take root and blossom into fantastic results.

CANDID CORNICE BLACK AND WHITE STRIPED CURTAINS TOPPED WITH A MATCHING PAINTED CORNICE PUNCTUATE THIS SOPHISTICATED SOUTHWESTERN-STYLE BEDROOM WITH GRAPHIC, FRESH FLAIR. THE SPECIAL TOUCH COMES FROM MOUNTING A FRAMED PRINT IN THE CENTER OF THE CORNICE. THE FEATURE DRAWS THE EYE UPWARD TO EMPHASIZE THE ROOM'S AIRY SENSE OF SPACE.

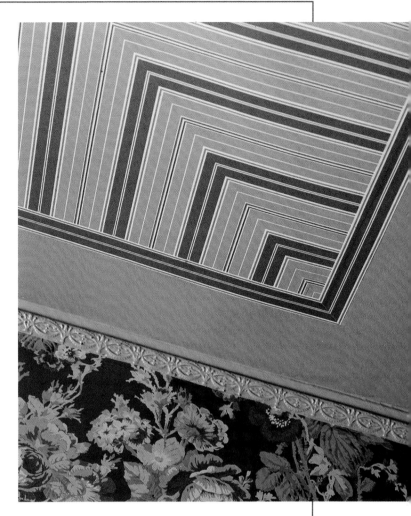

WILD ABOUT WALLPAPER

DON'T SHY AWAY FROM LAYERING STRONG PATTERNS, COLORS, AND TEXTURES. INDEED, NATURE PROVIDES ABUNDANT INSPIRATION FOR SUCH JUXTAPOSITIONS. IN THIS TROPICAL-LOOKING MORNING ROOM, RICH FLORAL WALLPAPER IN EARTHY TONES OF CHOCOLATE, GREEN, AND EGGPLANT CLIMBS THE WALLS TO MEET A CEILING THAT RESEMBLES PAINTED BEADED BOARD—ALSO WALLPAPER WITH STRIPES MITERED TO CREATE PERFECT CORNERS. WITH SUCH DRAMATIC PATTERNS IN THE ROOM, THE WINDOW FRAMES AND DOOR ARE SIMPLY PAINTED DEEP GREEN TO CONTINUE THE BACKGROUND COLOR OF THE WALLPAPER.

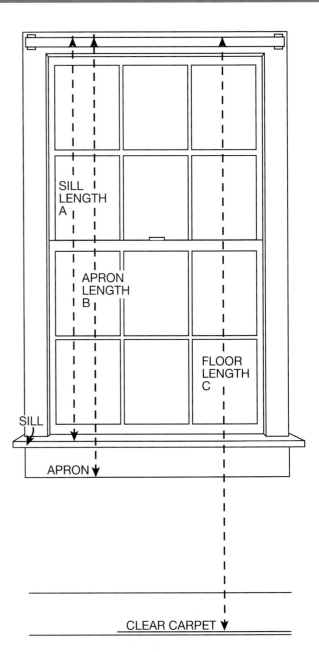

SILL
LENGTH
A

APRON
LENGTH
B

FLOOR
LENGTH
C

SILL

APRON

CLEAR CARPET

Measuring Windows

Nothing is as frustrating as ordering curtains or shutters only to find that they don't fit. The easiest solution is to have a professional come to your home and do the measuring. In fact, many installation companies will not order window treatments without premeasuring the windows themselves.

However, many companies that sell blinds and window treatments at a discount do not provide this service, leaving accurate measuring up to you. If you don't get it right, you may not be able to return the treatments even if they don't fit.

HERE ARE TIPS TO HELP YOU WITH MEASURING.

1 Use these terms and lengths when measuring for ready-made or catalog-order treatments. For example, cafe curtains usually break at the sill (sill length A); some country-style curtains may break at or below the apron (apron length B). Note also that floor length (C) refers to the measurement from the top of the window or above the window trim to the floor.

2 To ensure accuracy, use a steel measuring tape. Decide whether you want your treatments to be an inside mount, the most common type of treatment and one that fits inside your window, or an outside mount that covers your window. Measure accordingly.

3 For an inside mount, measure the opening width at the top, middle, and bottom, recording the narrowest measurement. Do the same for the length, recording the longest measurement. Round to the closest ⅛ inch.

4 For an outside mount, measure the width of the window opening and add at least 3 inches to each side of the window opening if there is room. Measure the length of the window opening and add at least 2 inches in height for hardware and any overlap.

5 To measure the drop for draperies, measure your windows from where you intend to install the rod to where you want draperies to fall. For width, measure the full length of the rod. To calculate the length of a decorative scarf or a single fabric piece, measure the distance from the bottom of the drapery ring or the top of the rod to the desired length of the scarf. Multiply that measurement by 2 and add 10 inches to each side if you want the fabric to puddle on the floor. Measure the width of the area to be covered and add that figure to the length for the total yardage needed.

Fabric Planner

The fabric you choose for window treatments can affect everything from the style of your decor to the mood of the room. The many options give you an array of choices but also challenge you to narrow your decision to the appropriate fabric. This summary provides information to help you make your selection.

CHINTZ is a lightweight cotton that drapes well. Some types, however, have a heavy glaze finish that often seems stiff. Prices vary according to the complexity of the pattern and the number of colors. Use lining with chintz and other printed cottons or cotton blends to avoid sun damage.

LINEN, which is spun from the flax plant, creates strong, smooth, sophisticated fabrics. Linen creases and drapes stiffly so is frequently blended with cotton for added softness. Raw linen is prized for its nubby texture.

DAMASK is woven of silk, cotton, linen, and other fibers. It is distinguished by its contrasting satiny and matte surfaces created by different weaves. Heavy damasks are best for grand sweeping statements, such as full draperies that show off the sumptuous fabric.

POLYESTER blends with other fibers without compromising their best features. It is wrinkle-resistant, resilient, stain-resistant, and able to retain pressed-in pleats.

RAYON dyes beautifully and drapes well, making it a good candidate for soft window dressings. It also blends well with natural or other synthetic fibers to retain color.

SHEERS include any soft, translucent fabric, such as muslin, voile, or lace. Varying in opacity, these textiles gently diffuse light. Pair them with shades or blinds for privacy.

SILK makes soft and graceful window dressings. This fabric absorbs dye well, making the colors bright and clear. However, sun can fade or weaken silk, so line and interline silk treatments and block the sun with shades or blinds.

TAFFETA, a crisp, plain-weave fabric, feels almost stiff enough to stand alone. In some window coverings, this is an asset. Taffeta retains its shape with little support.

TOILE refers to a tightly woven cotton, usually with a pictorial scene printed in one color. As with all cottons and linens, ward off sun damage with a lining.

WOOL is hard-wearing and durable and hangs in full, loose folds, making it perfect for long draperies and blocking heat and cold. It can be pricey and most often has to be dry-cleaned.

VELVET, an elegant fabric, blocks drafts and light with ease. The price of velvet depends on the fibers—velvet can be woven of silk, cotton, linen, rayon, wool, or even mohair.

WALL PLANNER

HOW MUCH PAINT DO YOU NEED?

1 Begin by calculating the square footage of the surfaces to be painted. Measure the length and width of the room to determine the perimeter. For example, if the room is 13 feet wide and 18 feet long, its perimeter is 13+13+18+18=62 feet.

2 Multiply the perimeter by the room's height to get square feet of wall space. If the room is 8 feet high, then its square footage is 62×8=496 square feet.

3 Subtract 21 square feet for each standard door and 15 square feet for each standard window. If the room has one door and three windows: 21+15+15+15=66 square feet. The final calculation is 496–66=430 square feet of wall space.

4 Divide the square feet of wall space by 300, the square footage easily covered by a gallon of interior paint, to get the number of gallons needed. In this example, you need 1 gallon plus nearly 2 quarts to paint the walls, so round up the amount to 1 gallon and 2 quarts. To calculate how much paint you need to cover the ceiling, multiply the length by the width to get the area in square feet, then divide by 300. A 13×18-foot room has a 234-square-foot ceiling, so 1 gallon of paint would suffice.

HOW MUCH WALLPAPER DO YOU NEED?

Wallcoverings are priced and measured by the single roll but packaged in double- or triple-rolls. To determine the amount you need, multiply the height of the wall by the width, or the perimeter of the room, then divide by 25, which is the usable square footage of a single roll. For example, 8-foot×12-foot perimeter=96 total feet, divided by 25 = 3.84 rolls of wallpaper. Because you can't buy 3.84 rolls of wallpaper, round up to the next even number, 4. Do not deduct for doors and windows because you'll need the extra square footage to account for pattern repeats. If you choose wallpaper with a pattern repeat over 18 inches, divide by 22 square feet instead of 25 feet.

Find Your Style

Better Homes and Gardens.

window *treatment* FOR EVERY ROOM

Better Homes and Gardens.
kids' rooms
decorating ideas
under
$50

Better Homes and Gardens.
decorating ideas
under
$50

quick updates
to what you
already own

Better Homes and Gardens.
new *cottage*

new Better Homes and Gardens.
decorating
book

Better **Homes** and Gardens®

The elements of your style...
can be found in great decorating books from
Better Homes and Gardens®—wherever books are sold.